THE OFFICIAL MANCHESTER UNITED ANNUAL 2008

BEN HIBBS and **PAUL DAVIES**

CONTENTS

INSIDE UNITED

MANCHESTER UNITED

The Boss

SIR ALEX'S SILVERWARE   In his 21 years in the Old Trafford hot-seat the Scot has won 26 trophies...

FA PREMIER LEAGUE x9
1992/93, 1993/94, 1995/96, 1996/97, 1998/99, 1999/2000, 2000/01, 2002/03, 2006/07 ▶

FA CUP x5
1990, 1994, 1996, 1999 ▶, 2004

LEAGUE CUP x2
1992, 2006 ▼

WELCOME TO MANCHESTER UNITED ANNUAL 2008 WITH THE CLUB ONCE AGAIN PREMIER LEAGUE CHAMPIONS

SEASON 2006/07 WAS A TRULY MEMORABLE ONE FOR THE PLAYERS, STAFF AND SUPPORTERS AND THE FUTURE PROMISES TO BE JUST AS THRILLING. BUT BEFORE LOOKING AHEAD TO WHAT LIES IN STORE FOR THIS CAMPAIGN IT IS ONLY RIGHT THAT I SHOULD CONCENTRATE ON THE TREMENDOUS ACHIEVEMENT OF LAST SEASON.

Every player contributed to the title success, from senior players like Ryan Giggs and Paul Scholes to newcomers like Michael Carrick and Nemanja Vidic, and youngsters like Wayne Rooney, Darren Fletcher and John O'Shea. Some people forgot how young they were when they started coming into the side, and we still haven't seen them in full bloom yet because they are only just starting to mature.

Special mention must go to Cristiano Ronaldo, too, who swept the board as the Professional Footballers' Association and the Football Writers' Player of the Year, plus being named Sir Matt Busby and Players' Player of the Year in our own club awards. For a winger to score 23 goals, it was an outstanding contribution.

However, although our Portuguese youngster scored heavily in the individual stakes, I cannot emphasise enough that the key to our success was based on the team ethic.

We have a lot of major stars and strong personalities at the club these days but we don't have any inflated egos. I strongly believe that if they stay together the whole team is going to get better and better. They have already proved themselves by winning the Premier League and hopefully will underline their quality by going on to even greater heights. The experience of Scholes, Giggs and Gary Neville will be vital over the next two seasons as the younger players develop, and with some major signings only strengthening us further, there's every reason to be confident because I believe this team has a very bright future.

Enjoy the read.

Sir Alex Ferguson

UEFA CHAMPIONS LEAGUE x1
1999 ◄

EUROPEAN CUP-WINNERS' CUP x1
1991 ◄

FA COMMUNITY SHIELD x6
1990 (joint holders), 1993, 1994, 1996, 1997, 2003

UEFA SUPER CUP x1
1991

INTER-CONTINENTAL CUP x1
1999

BEFORE UNITED'S FIRST GAME OF THE NEW SEASON AGAINST FULHAM, SIR ALEX FERGUSON ANNOUNCED, 'WE KNOW THE TARGET WE MUST AIM FOR THIS SEASON, AND TO REACH IT WE MUST HIT THE GROUND RUNNING.'

THE TARGET WAS TO WRESTLE THE PREMIERSHIP TITLE FROM CHELSEA'S GRASP, AND HITTING THE GROUND RUNNING MEANT GETTING OFF TO A FLYING START. AND UNITED CERTAINLY DID THAT.

AUGUST 2006

Sun 20	Fulham	H	Won	5-1
Wed 23	Charlton Athletic	A	Won	3-0
Sat 26	Watford	A	Won	2-1

Old Trafford buzzed with anticipation as the Reds lined up against Chris Coleman's Fulham side – and the Cottagers were simply blown away. Louis Saha, Wayne Rooney and Cristiano Ronaldo added to Ian Pearce's own goal to all but end the match as a contest inside the first 20 minutes. Even Rio Ferdinand's own goal couldn't dampen the mood as Rooney made it 5-1 in the second half. The result sent a message to the rest of the Premiership: United are a force to be reckoned with.

And Sir Alex's men continued that fine start with a 3-0 win over Charlton at the Valley, thanks to goals from Darren Fletcher, Saha and Ole Gunnar Solskjaer.

But if the first two games had seen exciting football and plenty of goals, the third was a scrappy fight against newly promoted Watford. It wasn't a classic, but goals from Mikael Silvestre and the in-form Ryan Giggs proved that the Reds know how to battle to win matches.

KEY STATS:
in August...

19,453
attendance against Watford, United's lowest league crowd in 2006/07

7
number of different scorers in the first three games of the season

It took the Reds just
19 minutes
to go 4-0 up against Fulham

SILENCING THE BOOS

After England were knocked out in the quarter-finals of the World Cup by Portugal, a game that also saw Wayne Rooney sent off after a clash with Ricardo Carvalho, many Three Lions' supporters blamed Cristiano Ronaldo. Despite his every touch being booed in the early matches of the season, the winger responded in the only way he knows how – using his talent on the pitch.

SEPTEMBER 2006

Sat 9	Tottenham Hotspur	H	Won	1-0
Sun 17	Arsenal	H	Lost	0-1
Sat 23	Reading	A	Drawn	1-1

United's perfect start to the season came to an end in September, but the Reds still remained in touch with leaders Chelsea.

Following a two-week international break, Sir Alex's men began the month against Spurs at Old Trafford, a game that pitted new signing Michael Carrick against his former club. Picking up where the team had left off in August United secured a 1-0 win, the goal coming from Ryan Giggs, who headed in the rebound after Paul Robinson had pawed away a Cristiano Ronaldo free-kick.

Eight days later the Reds were back at Old Trafford facing north London opposition again, this time it was Arsenal. Unfortunately, a tired looking Reds – playing their third game in eight days after a midweek Champions League clash with Celtic – slipped to their first defeat of the season. 'We let ourselves down with our passing and movement,' said Gary Neville of the 1-0 loss, 'it wasn't crisp, quick or accurate enough.'

Cristiano Ronaldo had been in sparkling form in the opening weeks of 2006/07 and was the star man again when Sir Alex's side took on Reading at the Madejski Stadium. A Kevin Doyle penalty put the home side ahead only for the Portuguese winger to produce a moment of magic, cutting into the penalty area from the left to shoot home. But it ended a mixed month for the Reds.

Michael Carrick shows excellent close control during United's 1-0 victory against his old club Tottenham at Old Trafford.

KEY STATS: in September...

number of goals scored by United by the end of September	**12**
20	number of players Sir Alex used in September's three Premiership matches
minute in which Ronaldo scored United's equaliser at Reading	**73**

75,595
fans saw the Reds take on Arsenal at Old Trafford

FLYING RYAN

In September Ryan Giggs proved himself as nimble and skilful as ever. The Welshman may have been only two months short of his 33rd birthday but he rolled back the years with a stunning display – and a goal – against Spurs.

OCTOBER 2006

Sun 1	Newcastle United	H	Won	2-0
Sat 14	Wigan Athletic	A	Won	3-1
Sun 22	Liverpool	H	Won	2-0
Sat 28	Bolton Wanderers	A	Won	4-0

After a slight stumble in September, the Reds needed to get back on track, and they did exactly that, kicking off October with a 2-0 win over Newcastle, Ole Gunnar Solskjaer grabbing both goals at Old Trafford.

Then came a trip to Wigan, and United fell behind after just six minutes. It stayed that way until the hour mark, but with Ryan Giggs on at half-time the Reds pushed for victory. Nemanja Vidic grabbed his first goal for the club with a powerful header after 62 minutes, then four minutes later Louis Saha put the Reds in front, before Solskjaer made certain with a third goal in injury-time.

Next came Liverpool, and a 500th United appearance for Paul Scholes. It was fitting that the midfield maestro opened the scoring in a match that also saw Rio Ferdinand get his first goal of the campaign, brilliantly bringing the ball down before smashing it into the top corner to complete a 2-0 win.

But the best was saved till last as Bolton were on the end of a true football masterclass. Rooney

An explosive performance against Bolton brought Wayne Rooney his first Premiership hat-trick. Here he outpaces the Bolton defence to finish the scoring with an unstoppable right-footer.

ended a run of ten games without a goal with his first ever Premiership hat-trick, adding to Cristiano Ronaldo's strike, as United moved back to the top of the Premiership.

Unbeaten, 11 goals scored and just one conceded, it was a good month for the Reds, and Sir Alex knew it, 'There is spirit and belief in the dressing room that tells me we'll be having a real go for trophies this season'.

KEY STATS: in October...

11	**16**
goals scored	players used in the league

199,352 fans watched United play

number of goals scored by Wayne Rooney against Bolton	**3**

MILESTONE MOMENT

After four months out at the end of 2005/06 with a serious eye injury, everyone was delighted just to have Paul Scholes back. But his form in 2006/07 proved he's still among the best midfielders in the world. If proof were needed of his value to the team, he opened the scoring against Liverpool in his 500th appearance for the Reds.

NOVEMBER 2006

Sat 4	Portsmouth	H	Won	3-0
Sat 11	Blackburn Rovers	A	Won	1-0
Sat 18	Sheffield United	A	Won	2-1
Sun 26	Chelsea	H	Drawn	1-1
Wed 29	Everton	H	Won	3-0

The Reds went into November as Premiership leaders looking to increase their advantage. Four wins and one draw – against champions Chelsea – ensured that target was achieved.

United's first league action saw them play host to Portsmouth on a very special day for Sir Alex. The Reds' boss was keen to play down the 20th anniversary of his arrival at Old Trafford but the fans and media ensured it was a day of celebration. The players responded too, running out 3-0 winners with goals from Louis Saha, Cristiano Ronaldo and Nemanja Vidic.

A week later the Reds registered another three points, this time at the tough venue of Blackburn's Ewood Park. On a rain-soaked afternoon United earned a hard-fought 1-0 victory, courtesy of a second-half volley from Saha.

Sir Alex's men were on the road again seven days later, this time crossing the Pennines to beat Sheffield United 2-1 thanks to a Wayne Rooney brace, before returning to Old Trafford for back-to-back matches against José Mourinho's men and Everton.

United went into the top-of-the table clash against Chelsea with a three-point advantage. It ended that way too – Saha's stunning long-range strike cancelled out by a second-half Ricardo Carvalho header for the visitors in a 1-1 draw.

Three days later and the Reds were back to winning ways as goals from Ronaldo, Patrice Evra (his first for the club) and John O'Shea saw off Everton in a comfortable 3-0 win.

Goals from Patrice Evra (below left), John O'Shea (right) and Ronaldo saw United to a comfortable 3-0 win over Everton.

20 YEARS AT THE TOP

Sir Alex Ferguson celebrated 20 years as United manager in the game against Portsmouth and his side marked the occasion with a 3-0 victory. 'Many things have contributed to the success over the last 20 years,' said the United boss, 'but I must thank the supporters who've shown me great loyalty which I have always appreciated'.

DECEMBER 2006

Sat 2	Middlesbrough	A	Won	2-1
Sat 9	Manchester City	H	Won	3-1
Sun 17	West Ham United	A	Lost	0-1
Sat 23	Aston Villa	A	Won	3-0
Tue 26	Wigan Athletic	H	Won	3-1
Sat 30	Reading	H	Won	3-2

With six league games December marked United's busiest month of the campaign, and the Reds certainly got into the festive spirit, treating fans to a mammoth 14 goals in the final month of 2006.

Sir Alex's side began away at Middlesbrough with a seventh win in eight games – Louis Saha converting from the penalty spot after Boro keeper Mark Schwarzer had fouled Cristiano Ronaldo. James Morrison equalised for the home team, but Darren Fletcher's header gave the Reds a valuable victory in a tight match.

Despite the presence of five Middlesbrough defenders Darren Fletcher heads United to victory in a close encounter at the Riverside.

The following weekend saw local derbies for both United and title rivals Chelsea, against Manchester City and Arsenal respectively. United won 3-1 thanks to Ronaldo, Saha and Wayne Rooney, while Arsenal did United a rare favour and held Chelsea to a draw.

However, the tables were turned a week later as José Mourinho's men came from 2-1 down against Everton to win 3-2, moments before United kicked off against West Ham. Didier Drogba's last-gasp winner seemed to affect the Reds, who suffered a frustrating 1-0 loss in Alan Curbishley's first game in charge at Upton Park, reducing United's lead to just two points.

But Sir Alex's side delivered the perfect response, beating Aston Villa 3-0, Wigan 3-1 and Reading 3-2 over Christmas – Ronaldo notching an incredible two goals in each of the three games – to put the Reds on 54 points compared to Chelsea's 48 going into the new year.

HIT FOR SIX

In such a tiring month, players need to call upon every ounce of energy and determination. Nobody did that more than Cristiano Ronaldo, scorer of six goals in three games, most notably registering twice within four minutes of coming on as a half-time substitute against Wigan on Boxing Day.

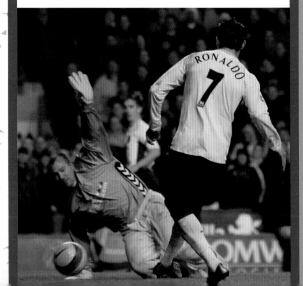

JANUARY 2007

Mon 1	Newcastle United	A	Drawn	2-2
Sat 13	Aston Villa	H	Won	3-1
Sun 21	Arsenal	A	Lost	1-2
Wed 31	Watford	H	Won	4-0

Despite losing to rivals Arsenal at the Emirates Stadium, United maintained their six-point lead over Chelsea at the end of the first month of the New Year.

The first action of 2007 saw United take on Newcastle at St James' Park. Despite dominating possession for long periods of the match – and two goals from Paul Scholes – the Reds were held 2-2 by the home side. Fortunately, Chelsea were unable to take advantage of United's slip as they were held 0-0 by Aston Villa.

Two weeks later it was United's turn to take on the Villans and goals from Michael Carrick (his first for the club), Ji-sung Park (his first of the season) and Cristiano Ronaldo (his 12th league goal) ensured a comfortable 3-1 win.

Next came one of the matches Sir Alex had pinpointed as the toughest remaining fixtures of the season – a trip to Arsenal. The Reds took the lead early in the second half, Wayne Rooney diving to nod in the first headed goal of his United career. But, sadly, just as it seemed the Reds were cruising to victory, the Gunners caught Sir Alex's men with a sucker-punch of two goals in the final seven minutes.

Getting back to winning ways was now the priority, and against Watford that was achieved through goals from Ronaldo, Rooney, Larsson and an own goal, to maintain United's top-of-the-table advantage.

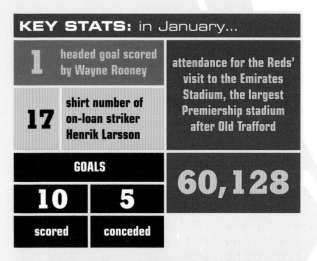

KEY STATS: in January...

1 headed goal scored by Wayne Rooney	**60,128** attendance for the Reds' visit to the Emirates Stadium, the largest Premiership stadium after Old Trafford
17 shirt number of on-loan striker Henrik Larsson	

GOALS	
10 scored	**5** conceded

CARRICK CRACKER

Michael Carrick is not noted for scoring goals, so he was understandably delighted when he opened his account for United at Old Trafford. His sweetly struck half-volley from the edge of the box helped the Reds to a 3-1 win over Aston Villa, and the midfielder later said, 'The way we play allows me to get forward more – it's nice to get among the goals.'

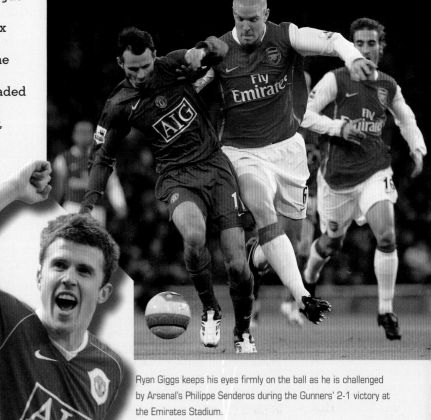

Ryan Giggs keeps his eyes firmly on the ball as he is challenged by Arsenal's Philippe Senderos during the Gunners' 2-1 victory at the Emirates Stadium.

FEBRUARY 2007

Sun 4	Tottenham Hotspur	A	Won	4-0
Sat 10	Charlton Athletic	H	Won	2-0
Sat 24	Fulham	A	Won	2-1

The Reds started February with a thumping 4-0 away win against Tottenham – the perfect response to Chelsea having briefly cut United's lead at the top to three points with their win over Charlton. Some had predicted the Reds would struggle at White Hart Lane. But Cristiano Ronaldo put United in front from the penalty spot, before Nemanja Vidic, Paul Scholes and Ryan Giggs completed the rout. United even managed to keep a clean sheet when John O'Shea had to go in goal to replace the injured Edwin van der Sar, who suffered a broken nose in a challenge with Robbie Keane.

Ronaldo starts the rout from the penalty spot against Tottenham at White Hart Lane. United's 4-0 victory in the capital sent out a clear warning to title rivals Chelsea that this time the Reds meant business.

Although Ronaldo stole the headlines with his late winner against Fulham, United's defence, particularly Nemanja Vidic, was among the meanest in the league this season. United conceded only one goal in the Premiership during February.

A routine 2-0 win over Charlton followed with a goal in each half from Ji-sung Park and Darren Fletcher. But it was the final match in February that produced one of the season's crucial moments. The game against Fulham started badly as the home side took the lead after 17 minutes through Brian McBride. Ryan Giggs levelled before the break with an excellent volley, but Fulham stood firm and looked to have earned a draw, seriously damaging United's title ambitions.

However, like the very best teams, the best players never give in. And with two minutes remaining Ronaldo came up with the goods. Receiving the ball inside his own half, he skipped past two challenges before bursting into the box, beating another defender and firing his shot into the far corner… a moment of sheer magic!

KEY STATS: in February…

88 minutes on the clock as Ronaldo scored the winner against Fulham

number of points United led Chelsea by at the end of February	number of passes attempted by Paul Scholes in the Premiership this season, 91 per cent of which reached their target
9	**1,542**

SILVER IN SIGHT?

'Mourinho, are you listening?
You better keep that trophy glistening.
We'll be back in May, to take it away,
walking in a Fergie wonderland.'

Though the title race was by no means over at this point, there was growing confidence among United's supporters.

MARCH 2007

Sat 3	Liverpool	A	Won	1-0
Sat 17	Bolton Wanderers	H	Won	4-1
Sat 31	Blackburn Rovers	H	Won	4-1

For United fans there are few things quite as enjoyable as watching the team beat fierce north-west rivals Liverpool. When the winning goal comes in injury-time at the Kop end of Anfield to keep the Reds top of the Premiership... well, that's the stuff dreams are made of. And that's exactly what happened in the Reds' first Premiership match of March.

Another late winner and another three points: John O'Shea celebrates with Michael Carrick in front of the Kop at Anfield after giving United an important victory against Liverpool.

United followed up the thrilling late win at Fulham in February with another memorable victory. Outplayed for long periods, the Reds held off Liverpool's late pressure to snatch victory. Deep in stoppage time Cristiano Ronaldo sent in a dangerous low free-kick that opposition keeper Pepe Reina could only push out and substitute John O'Shea scored on the rebound.

Confidence was surging through the United team now and consecutive victories against Lancashire neighbours Bolton and Blackburn kept the Reds in pole position to win the title. However, the games could not have been more different.

Ji-sung Park and Wayne Rooney shared out the goals evenly as United scored four against Bolton for the second time this season.

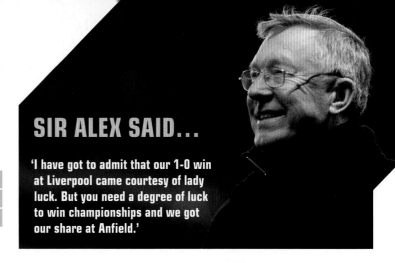

SIR ALEX SAID...

'I have got to admit that our 1-0 win at Liverpool came courtesy of lady luck. But you need a degree of luck to win championships and we got our share at Anfield.'

Wayne Rooney and Korean international Ji-sung Park scored two each in the thrashing of Bolton. But against Mark Hughes' Blackburn things were considerably harder. It all went Rovers' way after taking the lead through Matt Derbyshire and United saw Nemanja Vidic stretchered off with a shoulder injury.

The second half was a different story entirely. In what Sir Alex described as United's 'best display of the season' Paul Scholes scored a superb equaliser, paving the way for further strikes from Michael Carrick, Park and Ole Gunnar Solskjaer. It kept United very much on course for silverware.

KEY STATS: in March...

90 minutes on the clock as John O'Shea scored the winner at Anfield

number of league goals scored — **9**

6 players scored them: Park (3), Rooney (2), Carrick, Scholes, Solskjaer, O'Shea

2 12.45pm Saturday kick-offs

9 substitutions made by Sir Alex

76,098 fans watched the game against Blackburn – the highest ever attendance for a United match at Old Trafford

11

APRIL 2007

Sat 7	Portsmouth	A	Lost	1-2
Tue 17	Sheffield United	H	Won	2-0
Sat 21	Middlesbrough	H	Drawn	1-1
Sat 28	Everton	A	Won	4-2

United arrived at Portsmouth's Fratton Park on the back of seven straight wins, but the midweek Champions League loss away to AS Roma having been down to ten men for much of the match, had taken its toll on Sir Alex's team. An off-colour United lost 2-1 as a Matthew Taylor strike and a Rio Ferdinand own goal cancelled out John O'Shea's effort.

Relegation-threatened Sheffield United posed the next hurdle, but after beating Roma 7-1 in Europe and Watford 4-1 in the FA Cup the Reds were full of confidence, and Michael Carrick and Wayne Rooney made sure of three points. However, it was a nervous United back

It's that man again: Ronaldo heads the ball down before former Red Phil Neville inadvertently turns the ball into his own net to level the scores at 2-2 midway through the second half away at Everton...

at Old Trafford four days later for a 1-1 draw against a Middlesbrough side determined to gain revenge after league and cup defeats earlier in the campaign.

Cue one of the season's most dramatic afternoons as United kicked off against Everton at Goodison Park at the same time as Chelsea met Bolton at Stamford Bridge. The Blues came from a goal down to lead 2-1, while the Reds worryingly slipped 2-0 behind. But the Reds fought back, as did Bolton. Kevin Davies equalised for the Wanderers, while John O'Shea snatched a priceless goal midway through the second half. Ex-Red Phil Neville turned the ball into his own net to haul United level a few minutes before Wayne Rooney's fine finish and a late Chris Eagles strike claimed all three points on Merseyside. The Reds had taken a big step closer to the title.

... 15 minutes later, with United now 3-2 ahead through Wayne Rooney's fine finish, Chris Eagles races into the Everton penalty area and strikes a low shot into the net to score his first goal for United, secure three precious points and all but seal the title.

KEY STATS: in April...

Chris Eagles registered his ever goal for the club against Everton	**1st**	
85 number of points United had at the end of the month	Chelsea's total at the same point	
	80	
2	goals scored by John O'Shea, taking him to four for the season so far	

SIR ALEX SAID...

'I feel the momentum is with us, particularly with Chelsea drawing against Bolton. We have a five-point lead and a marvellous chance of winning the title with just three games left.'

MAY 2007

Sat 5	Manchester City	A	Won	1-0
Wed 9	Chelsea	A	Drawn	0-0
Sun 13	West Ham United	H	Lost	0-1

In the Manchester derby it was Edwin van der Sar's turn to shine as he kept out Darius Vassell's second-half spot kick to secure three points thanks to a first-half penalty from Ronaldo. Now all United had to do was wait…

April's final act, the dramatic, almost unbelievable victory at Everton, had left United on the brink of a ninth Premiership title. Yet nobody at Old Trafford was taking anything for granted, not with a tricky trip to Manchester City, a potential title-decider with Chelsea at Stamford Bridge and a visit from a West Ham side fighting for their Premier League survival.

An energy-sapping trip to Milan in midweek was hardly the ideal preparation for a Manchester derby but the Reds came through, just, thanks to a Ronaldo penalty and an Edwin van der Sar penalty save. The Portuguese star coolly despatched his kick, awarded after he'd been fouled by Michael Ball, and United's Dutch stopper kept his nerve to keep out a tame Darius Vassell shot to ensure a crucial, hopefully title-clinching 1-0 win. 'It wasn't a great performance, but derby games can be like that. The courage we showed was fantastic,' said a jubilant, and relieved, Sir Alex.

Just over 24 hours later the United boss and his players, not to mention fans all over the world, were celebrating again – this time a ninth Premiership title and 16th league success. As Chelsea could only manage a 1-1 draw with Arsenal at the Emirates, United were once again confirmed kings of English football.

Not even a 0-0 draw at Chelsea three days later and final day defeat to West Ham at Old Trafford could dampen Red spirits as Ryan Giggs and Gary Neville jointly lifted the Premiership trophy. What a moment, what a season, what a team!

KEY STATS: in May…

number of people who saw United presented with the Premiership trophy at the match against West Ham	**75,927**
83	total number of league goals scored by United this season
United's final title-winning points margin over Chelsea	**6**
17	goals were scored by Cristiano Ronaldo, the Reds' top scorer in the Premiership

CHAMPIONS AGAIN

The final game in April had seen United move a step closer to the title, victory in the Manchester derby moved it closer still and a draw for Chelsea at Arsenal confirmed it… United were champions, Sir Alex and Ryan Giggs both winning the Premiership for the ninth time. Altogether now, as the Stretford End sang during the final league game of the season, 'Champions, champions, champions!'

CHAMPIONS
OF THE PREMIER LEAGUE

AT THE START OF THE 2006/07 SEASON UNITED HAD ONE MAIN TARGET – WINNING BACK THE PREMIER LEAGUE TITLE – AND AS WE HAVE SEEN ACHIEVED THAT GOAL IN A THRILLING CAMPAIGN. AFTER OVERCOMING A DETERMINED CHELSEA SIDE UNITED WON A 16TH LEAGUE CHAMPIONSHIP. FROM GIGGS COLLECTING A RECORD NINTH WINNERS' MEDAL TO ROONEY AND RONALDO EARNING THEIR FIRST, THE CELEBRATIONS AT OLD TRAFFORD IN MAY PROVED A GREAT MOMENT FOR ALL CONCERNED...

'IT'S BEEN A FANTASTIC SEASON FOR OUR CLUB, FOR EVERY ONE OF US... THE SUPPORTERS, THE STAFF, THE PLAYERS, I CAN'T SPEAK HIGHLY ENOUGH OF THEM. IT'S BEEN A WONDERFUL YEAR.'
SIR ALEX FERGUSON

'I'M NOT THINKING OF IT AS THE NINTH PREMIERSHIP TROPHY I'VE WON, I'M JUST GLAD TO HAVE WON THE LEAGUE THIS SEASON HAVING GONE THREE YEARS WITHOUT IT. THE FACT WE HAVE THE TITLE BACK MEANS MORE THAN ANY PERSONAL ACHIEVEMENT.'
RYAN GIGGS

'WINNING THE LEAGUE IS AS HARD AS EVER. YOU HAVE TO SAY IT'S THE BEST LEAGUE IN THE WORLD, AND WE'VE WON IT.'
GARY NEVILLE

'IT'S A MASSIVE TOURNAMENT FOR US TO WIN. WE'VE HAD 38 TOUGH GAMES SO TO COME OUT ON TOP OF THAT LEAGUE IS GREAT FOR US. HOPEFULLY WE WON'T HAVE TO WAIT FOR ANOTHER FOUR YEARS TO WIN IT AGAIN.'
WAYNE ROONEY

'THIS FEELING, THIS EXPERIENCE OF BEING CHAMPIONS IN ENGLAND IS AMAZING AND WE WANT TO WIN IT AGAIN NEXT SEASON.'
CRISTIANO RONALDO

'IT FEELS UNBELIEVABLE. I'VE COME A LONG WAY SINCE GETTING INJURED AGAINST LIVERPOOL LAST FEBRUARY. IT'S AN INCREDIBLE FEELING BEING OUT THERE LIFTING THE TROPHY. ALL THE HOURS PUT IN AT THE GYM, PLAYING FOR THE RESERVES – ALL THAT HARD WORK – TODAY IS WHAT IT'S ALL FOR.'
ALAN SMITH

'THE SPIRIT AT THE CLUB IS FANTASTIC. IT HAS PROBABLY BEEN THE KEY ATTRIBUTE THIS SEASON. ALL THE PLAYERS ENJOYED THE PREMIERSHIP SUCCESS IN THE SAME WAY. EVERYONE HAS GROWN UP THIS SEASON. THE EXPERIENCE, CONFIDENCE AND DESIRE HAVE BEEN BRILLIANT.'
CARLOS QUEIROZ

CHAMPIONS LEAGUE 2006/07

REACHING THE CHAMPIONS LEAGUE FINAL PROVED ONE STEP TOO FAR FOR SIR ALEX'S MEN, BUT UNITED'S PERFORMANCES SHOWED THAT FUTURE EUROPEAN SUCCESS MAY NOT BE FAR AWAY...

Group F

MANCHESTER UNITED 3
Saha (2), Solskjaer
CELTIC 2
Old Trafford, Wednesday 13 September 2006
A thrilling match saw United go 1-0 down, come back to lead 2-1, then concede again – all before half time. Fortunately, Ole Gunnar Solskjaer came up with the second-half winner to start the campaign off with a victory.

Above: Louis Saha's goals, including this one in the 3-1 win over Benfica at Old Trafford, played a big part in United's successful passage through the Group Stage of the competition.
Right: Paul Scholes was back to his very best in the 2006/07 Champions League campaign where his vision and skills were seen to be as sharp as ever.

SL BENFICA 0
MANCHESTER UNITED 1
Saha
Stadium of Light, Lisbon, Tuesday 26 September 2006
In December 2005, defeat to Benfica ended United's hopes at the group stage. This time, a well struck – albeit deflected – Louis Saha strike went some way to making up for that 2-1 loss.

MANCHESTER UNITED 3
Scholes, O'Shea, Richardson
FC COPENHAGEN 0
Old Trafford, Tuesday 17 October 2006
Captained by Wayne Rooney and driven by the skill of Paul Scholes, the Reds easily saw off the Danes.

FC COPENHAGEN 1
MANCHESTER UNITED 0
Parken Stadium, Copenhagen, Wednesday 1 November 2006
United struggled on a poor pitch at the Parken Stadium, former Aston Villa striker Marcus Allback hitting the winner on 73 minutes to shock the Reds.

CELTIC 1
MANCHESTER UNITED 0
Celtic Park, Glasgow, 21 November 2006
Despite controlling much of the match, the Reds missed a host of chances, including a Louis Saha penalty, and paid the price. Shunsuke Nakamura struck a wonderful free-kick on 81 minutes, meaning United had to avoid defeat in the final group match to reach the last 16.

MANCHESTER UNITED 3
Vidic, Giggs, Saha
SL BENFICA 1
Old Trafford, Wednesday 6 December 2006
This crucial match started badly for the Reds as chances went begging and Benfica took the lead. But Nemanja Vidic came to the rescue, smashing home a header just before half time. Now set on finishing the job, Ryan Giggs and Louis Saha grabbed second-half goals to see United through.

First Round, 1st leg

LILLE 0
MANCHESTER UNITED 1
Giggs
Felix-Bolleart Stadium, Lille, Tuesday 20 February 2007
Strong in midfield and organised at the back, Lille proved stubborn opponents and kept United at bay for most of the match. But the game took an astonishing twist on 84 minutes when Ryan Giggs' quickly taken free-kick beat Lille keeper Tony Sylva. Amazingly, in protest at the goal, the Lille players threatened to walk off. However, they eventually carried on and the Reds held out for the win.

First Round, 2nd leg

MANCHESTER UNITED 1
LILLE 0
Larsson
(United won 2-0 on aggregate)
Old Trafford, Wednesday 7 March 2007
United won this match through a combination of Cristiano Ronaldo's pace, Paul Scholes' guile and the goalscoring ability of Henrik Larsson in his last appearance for the Reds. The three players combined superbly to secure the win for United with 18 minutes left on the clock.

Quarter-final, 1st leg

AS ROMA 2
MANCHESTER UNITED 1
Rooney
Olympic Stadium, Rome, Wednesday 4 April 2007
With United a goal behind at half time and down to ten men after Paul Scholes' sending off, the Reds looked to be heading out of Europe. But Wayne Rooney's wonderful finish on the hour gave United hope, even if Roma did snatch a goal to win it on the night.

Quarter-final, 2nd leg

MANCHESTER UNITED 7
Carrick (2), Smith, Rooney, Ronaldo (2), Evra
(United won 8-3 on aggregate)
AS ROMA 1
Old Trafford, Tuesday 10 April 2007
A goal down from the first leg, United needed a big performance. They certainly got it. 'It was a fantastic display,' said Sir Alex after the game, 'the best European performance in my time here.' Fans lucky enough to witness this 7-1 thrashing

One moment of magic on a night of alchemy as Michael Carrick scores the sixth of United's seven goals against Roma.

are unlikely ever to forget what was a memorable and almost unbelievable occasion. The atmosphere was incredible and Roma were simply blown away. Michael Carrick, Alan Smith and Wayne Rooney all struck to put United 3-0 up inside 19 minutes. Ronaldo chipped in with a goal either side of half time, while Carrick added a second before Patrice Evra completed the scoring and a magical night at Old Trafford.

Semi-final, 1st leg

MANCHESTER UNITED 3
Ronaldo, Rooney (2)
AC MILAN 2
Old Trafford, Tuesday 24 April 2007
It seemed impossible to match the win over Roma, but although this was a much closer encounter, it had all the drama expected of a Champions League semi-final. Ronaldo put the Reds in front, then two other players took centre stage. AC Milan's Kaka scored twice to take the lead at half time. But the Brazilian's display was more than matched by Wayne Rooney. His second-half double, including an injury-time winner, gave United hope of a first final since 1999.

Semi-final, 2nd leg

AC MILAN 3
MANCHESTER UNITED 0
(United lost 5-3 on aggregate)
San Siro, Milan, Wednesday 2 May 2007
Hindered by injuries and showing tiredness from a tough Premiership campaign, the Reds suffered a frustrating night in Milan – a repeat of 2005's exit at the hands of the Italian club. But this United team continues to mature, and should Sir Alex face a third encounter with the Rossoneri, he will be confident of a different outcome.

FA CUP 2006/07
THE ROAD TO WEMBLEY

WITH UNITED GOING STRONG IN THREE COMPETITIONS IN 2006/07, WINNING THE TREBLE LOOKED INCREASINGLY POSSIBLE. THE FA CUP CAMPAIGN WAS CERTAINLY EVENTFUL AS THE REDS SCORED 15 GOALS ON THE ROAD TO THE FINAL AGAINST CHELSEA AT THE NEW WEMBLEY STADIUM...

Third Round

MANCHESTER UNITED 2
Larsson, Solskjaer
ASTON VILLA 1
Old Trafford, Sunday 7 January 2007

The Reds' 35-year-old loan striker Henrik Larsson opened the scoring on his debut, but it was another of the old guard, Ole Gunnar Solskjaer, that snatched the injury-time winner to kick-start United's cup run.

Fourth Round

MANCHESTER UNITED 2
Rooney (2)
PORTSMOUTH 1
Old Trafford, Saturday 27 January 2007

This was not a classic, but Wayne Rooney came off the bench to hit two match-winning goals, the second of which was sheer class. With David James expecting him to blast his shot from 25 yards, instead Rooney chipped it over the stranded keeper.

Ole Gunnar Solskjaer looks suitably pleased with himself after scoring his late winner against Aston Villa in the third round.

Fifth Round

MANCHESTER UNITED 1
Carrick
READING 1
Old Trafford, Saturday 17 February 2007

Michael Carrick's sweetly struck goal put the Reds in front, but Brynjar Gunnarsson's equaliser forced the tie back to the Madejski stadium for a replay.

Fifth Round, Replay

READING 2
MANCHESTER UNITED 3
Heinze, Saha, Solskjaer
Madejski Stadium, Tuesday 27 February 2007

United ran riot in the fifth round replay against Reading. Here Gabriel Heinze opens the scoring from 25-yards.

You're unlikely to see a more remarkable start to a match. Reading were stunned to find themselves 3-0 down after just six minutes as Gabriel Heinze, Louis Saha and Solskjaer all scored for the visitors. But Steve Coppell's side fought back with two goals to set up a tense finish. By the end United were clinging on but they did enough to win.

Ronaldo goes down under pressure from Boro defender Jonathan Woodgate. The flying winger got up, dusted himself down and scored from the resultant penalty to earn United a place in the semi-finals.

Wayne Rooney scored twice in United's 4-1 semi-final victory against Watford. He opened the scoring after six minutes with this blistering 20-yarder.

Sixth Round

MIDDLESBROUGH 2
MANCHESTER UNITED 2 Rooney, Ronaldo (pen)
Riverside Stadium, Saturday 10 March 2007
Despite going ahead through Rooney's strike, goals from Lee Cattermole and George Boateng looked to have ended the Reds' cup run. Cue a Cristiano Ronaldo equaliser from the penalty spot, forcing a replay at Old Trafford.

Sixth Round, Replay

MANCHESTER UNITED 1
Ronaldo (pen)
MIDDLESBROUGH 0
Old Trafford, Monday 19 March 2007
A determined Boro display made for a tough evening. And it took another penalty – United's third against Gareth Southgate's men in 2006/07 – from that boy Ronaldo (who scored the previous two) for the Reds to sneak through to the semi-finals.

Semi-final

MANCHESTER UNITED 4
Rooney (2), Ronaldo, Richardson
WATFORD 1
Villa Park, Saturday 14 April 2007
Having beaten AS Roma 7-1 in the Champions League just days before, United were full of confidence and in no mood to stop scoring at Villa Park. A double from Rooney, taking him to five in the competition, and one each

for Ronaldo and Kieran Richardson booked United a place in the final.

Final

CHELSEA 1
MANCHESTER UNITED 0
Wembley, Saturday 19 May 2007
With the title secured, Sir Alex was seeking a fourth double, and the impressive new Wembley stadium was the perfect stage. However, both teams looked tired, and on a slow pitch Chelsea's stifling style prevented the Reds playing their usual fast, attacking football. 'There was nothing between the teams,' said Sir Alex afterwards. True, but with 116 minutes on the clock and the match heading for penalties, Chelsea's Didier Drogba sneaked past United's defence and beat Edwin van der Sar to clinch the trophy. 'Neither team deserved to win or lose,' Sir Alex added. 'It's just really disappointing we were the ones that lost.'

CARLING CUP KIDS

The Reds' Carling Cup campaign was short (only two games), but sweet for several young players. Against Crewe, in the third round, five players – Phil Marsh, David Gray, Michael Barnes, Ryan Shawcross and Kieran Lee (left) – were all handed debuts. The latter made a telling contribution. On as a substitute, 19-year-old Lee struck the winning goal with just two minutes of extra-time remaining. However, a 1-0 defeat against Southend in the fourth round ended United's defence of the trophy they won in 2006.

Statistics 2006/07

AUGUST 2006

Sun 20	Prem	FULHAM	W 5-1	Saha, Rooney (2), Ronaldo, Pearce (og)
Wed 23	Prem	Charlton Athletic	W 3-0	Fletcher, Saha, Solskjaer
Sat 26	Prem	Watford	W 2-1	Silvestre, Giggs

SEPTEMBER 2006

Sat 9	Prem	TOTTENHAM HOTSPUR	W 1-0	Giggs
Wed 13	CL GpF	CELTIC	W 3-2	Saha (2), Solskjaer
Sun 17	Prem	ARSENAL	L 0-1	
Sat 23	Prem	Reading	D 1-1	Ronaldo
Tue 26	CL GpF	Benfica	W 1-0	Saha

OCTOBER 2006

Sun 1	Prem	NEWCASTLE UNITED	W 2-0	Solskjaer (2)
Sat 14	Prem	Wigan Athletic	W 3-1	Vidic, Saha, Solskjaer
Tue 17	CL GpF	FC COPENHAGEN	W 3-0	Scholes, O'Shea, Richardson
Sun 22	Prem	LIVERPOOL	W 2-0	Scholes, Ferdinand
Wed 25	CC Rd3	Crewe Alexandra	W 2-1	Solskjaer, Lee
Sat 28	Prem	Bolton Wanderers	W 4-0	Rooney (3), Ronaldo

NOVEMBER 2006

Wed 1	CL GpF	FC Copenhagen	L 0-1	
Sat 4	Prem	PORTSMOUTH	W 3-0	Saha, Ronaldo, Vidic
Tue 7	CC Rd4	Southend United	L 0-1	
Sat 11	Prem	Blackburn Rovers	W 1-0	Saha
Sat 18	Prem	Sheffield United	W 2-1	Rooney (2)
Tue 21	CL GpF	Celtic	L 0-1	
Sun 26	Prem	CHELSEA	D 1-1	Saha
Wed 29	Prem	EVERTON	W 3-0	Ronaldo, Evra, O'Shea

DECEMBER 2006

Sat 2	Prem	Middlesbrough	W 2-1	Saha, Fletcher
Wed 6	CL GpF	BENFICA	W 3-1	Vidic, Giggs, Saha
Sat 9	Prem	MANCHESTER CITY	W 3-1	Rooney, Saha, Ronaldo
Sun 17	Prem	West Ham United	L 0-1	
Sat 23	Prem	Aston Villa	W 3-0	Ronaldo (2), Scholes
Tue 26	Prem	WIGAN ATHLETIC	W 3-1	Ronaldo (2), Solskjaer
Sat 30	Prem	READING	W 3-2	Solskjaer, Ronaldo (2)

JANUARY 2007

Mon 1	Prem	Newcastle United	D 2-2	Scholes (2)
Sun 7	FAC Rd3	ASTON VILLA	W 2-1	Larsson, Solskjaer
Sat 13	Prem	ASTON VILLA	W 3-1	Park, Carrick, Ronaldo
Sun 21	Prem	Arsenal	L 1-2	Rooney
Sat 27	FAC Rd4	PORTSMOUTH	W 2-1	Rooney (2)
Wed 31	Prem	WATFORD	W 4-0	Ronaldo, Doyley (og), Larsson, Rooney

Top appearance maker and joint top-scorer Wayne Rooney gets away from Milan's Gennaro Gattuso during the Champions League semi-final second leg at the San Siro.

Joining Rooney on 23 goals for the season was Cristiano Ronaldo who won his first Premiership title since joining the club in 2003.

FEBRUARY 2007

Sun 4	Prem	Tottenham Hotspur	W 4-0	Ronaldo, Vidic, Scholes, Giggs
Sat 10	Prem	CHARLTON ATHLETIC	W 2-0	Park, Fletcher
Sat 17	FAC Rd5	READING	D 1-1	Carrick
Tue 20	CL Rd of 16	LOSC Lille	W 1-0	Giggs
Sat 24	Prem	Fulham	W 2-1	Giggs, Ronaldo
Tue 27	FAC Rd5/R	Reading	W 3-2	Heinze, Saha, Solskjaer

MARCH 2007

Sat 3	Prem	Liverpool	W 1-0	O'Shea
Wed 7	CL Rd of 16	LOSC LILLE	W 1-0	Larsson
Sat 10	FAC Rd6	Middlesbrough	D 2-2	Rooney, Ronaldo
Sat 17	Prem	BOLTON WANDERERS	W 4-1	Park (2), Rooney (2)
Mon 9	FAC Rd6/R	MIDDLESBROUGH	W 1-0	Ronaldo
Sat 31	Prem	BLACKBURN ROVERS	W 4-1	Scholes, Carrick, Park, Solskjaer

APRIL 2007

Wed 4	CL QF/1L	AS Roma	L 1-2	Rooney
Sat 7	Prem	Portsmouth	L 1-2	O'Shea
Tue 10	CL QF/2L	AS ROMA	W 7-1	Carrick (2), Smith, Rooney, Ronaldo (2), Evra
Sat 14	FAC SF	Watford	W 4-1	Rooney (2), Ronaldo, Richardson
Tue 17	Prem	SHEFFIELD UNITED	W 2-0	Rooney, Carrick
Sat 21	Prem	MIDDLESBROUGH	D 1-1	Richardson
Tue 24	CL SF/1L	AC MILAN	W 3-2	Ronaldo, Rooney (2)
Sat 28	Prem	Everton	W 4-2	O'Shea, P Neville (og), Rooney, Eagles

Alan Smith celebrated his first goal for United since November 2005 with this superb finish in the Champions League quarter-final against Roma at Old Trafford. The 7-1 scoreline was United's biggest win of the season.

MAY 2007

Wed 2	CL SF/2L	AC Milan	L 0-3	
Sat 5	Prem	Manchester City	W 1-0	Ronaldo
Wed 9	Prem	Chelsea	D 0-0	
Sun 13	Prem	WEST HAM UNITED	L 0-1	
Sat 19	FAC Final	Chelsea	L 0-1	aet

FACTS AND FIGURES

Total matches played 60
Premiership 38
Champions League 12
FA Cup 8
Carling Cup 2

TOP FIVE APPEARANCE MAKERS
Wayne Rooney 54 (4 as sub)
Cristiano Ronaldo 52 (4 as sub)
Michael Carrick 51 (4 as sub)
Rio Ferdinand 48 (1 as sub)
Edwin van der Sar 46

TOP FIVE GOALSCORERS
Cristiano Ronaldo 23
Wayne Rooney 23
Louis Saha 13
Ole Gunnar Solskjaer 11
Paul Scholes 7

PREMIERSHIP MEDALS WON
9 Ryan Giggs
7 Gary Neville, Paul Scholes
6 Ole Gunnar Solskjaer
4 Wes Brown, Mikael Silvestre
2 Rio Ferdinand, John O'Shea
1 Michael Carrick, Patrice Evra, Darren Fletcher, Gabriel Heinze, Tomasz Kuszczak, Henrik Larsson, Ji-sung Park, Kieran Richardson, Cristiano Ronaldo, Wayne Rooney, Louis Saha, Alan Smith, Edwin van der Sar, Nemanja Vidic

Total number of players used 31
Goals scored 123
Goals conceded 51
Clean sheets 21
Penalties for 6
Penalties against 4
Own goals 3

Longest winning sequence
7 games
Biggest win
7-1 (v AS Roma) (CL)
Highest attendance home
76,098 (v Blackburn Rovers)
Highest attendance away
89,826 (v Chelsea, Wembley)
Total number of fans that watched United in 2006/07
3,387,977

Edwin Van der Sar

Goalkeepers

BORN **29 OCTOBER 1970, VOORHOUT, HOLLAND**
SIGNED **1 JULY 2005, FROM FULHAM**
OTHER CLUBS **AJAX, JUVENTUS**
UNITED DEBUT **9 AUGUST 2005 v DEBRECENI (H)**
CHAMPIONS LEAGUE
INTERNATIONAL TEAM **HOLLAND**

'Edwin brings experience and calmness to the back four,' Sir Alex states proudly of United's commanding 6ft 6in goalkeeper. He's certainly lived up to those words in his first two seasons at Old Trafford since joining from Fulham in 2005.

The Dutchman's influence on United's title triumph in 2006/07 was strongly felt. The Reds' defence in general was outstanding, but when injuries struck towards the end of the campaign, van der Sar's reliability was vital. He missed just six league games all season, keeping 12 clean sheets. His £2 million transfer fee now appears money very well spent.

DID YOU KNOW?

In Manchester he is known as Ed or Edwin to his team-mates, but his Holland international colleagues call him 'Sar'. Away from football Edwin likes to play golf, tennis and squash but, despite being so tall, he isn't very good at basketball. 'Everyone thinks I must be brilliant at basketball because of my height, but I'm shocking!'

'I've made some nice saves throughout my career, but I'm still waiting to make my best one,' Edwin said recently, but his penalty stop against Manchester City in May 2007 must rank among the most important. With United winning 1-0, City earned a late penalty and the chance to damage United's title hopes. But a brilliant save with his legs from Darius Vassell's spot-kick ensured all three points – a crucial moment in beating Chelsea to the title.

Now with a Premiership winner's medal among his already impressive list of honours, the Dutchman will be hoping to add another Champions League trophy to the one he won with Ajax in 1995 before he calls an end to his glorious career.

Ben Foster

- **Born** 3 April 1983, Leamington Spa
- **Signed** 19 July 2005, from Stoke City
- **Fee** £1million
- **Other Clubs** Bristol City (loan), Wrexham (loan), Watford (loan)
- **International Team** England

Ben Foster waited two years to get his chance at United, now he's relishing the opportunity. The young goalkeeper, spotted during a loan spell with Wrexham, signed in summer 2005 from Stoke City, where he hadn't even played in the first team.

Almost immediately he was loaned to Watford for two years, where he saw the Hornets promoted from the Championship then relegated from the Premiership the following year. But he left his mark, with Watford boss Aidy Boothroyd tipping Foster to one day be 'the best in the world'. No wonder, he kept seven clean sheets despite Watford finishing bottom of the Premiership in 2006/07.

Arriving at United as an unknown, he returned from his loan spell at Watford as an England international. Knee surgery in the summer put his United career on hold again, but when he returns he will be a serious contender for the No.1 jersey.

Ben's debut at Old Trafford came 19 months after signing for the Reds, but it wasn't in a United shirt. Foster's England debut came against Spain at Old Trafford in February 2007.

Tomasz Kuszczak

- **Born** 20 March 1982, Krosno Ordzanskie, Poland
- **Signed** 10 August 2006, from West Bromwich Albion
- **Other Clubs** Hertha Berlin
- **United Debut** 17 September 2006 v Arsenal (H) Premiership
- **International Team** Poland

United signed Tomasz Kuszczak as cover for Edwin van der Sar, and he has proved to be more than capable of stepping in when required.

Reds' legend Peter Schmeichel was one of Tom's childhood idols, so he jumped at the chance to follow in the Dane's footsteps in summer 2006. 'It's always been my dream to play for United,' he said.

Kuszczak arrived knowing exactly what it takes to perform Old Trafford – in May 2005 he helped former club West Brom earn a 1-1 draw that kept the Baggies in the Premiership.

And he had to count on that experience on his United debut against Arsenal. With van der Sar suffering from illness, Kuszczak stepped in. He faced a Gunners penalty after just 12 minutes and saved brilliantly from Gilberto Silva. But his afternoon ended disappointingly as Emmanuel Adebayor won it for the Londoners late on. In 12 further appearances in 2006/07 he showed he is a reliable squad member.

Tomasz Kuszczak would get you a whopping 53 points on the scrabble board – a higher score than any other player in the Premiership.

Gary Neville
Defenders

MANCHESTER UNITED

BORN **18 FEBRUARY 1975, BURY**
SIGNED **8 JULY 1991, TRAINEE**
OTHER CLUBS **NONE**
UNITED DEBUT **16 SEPTEMBER 1992 v TORPEDO MOSCOW (H), UEFA CUP**
INTERNATIONAL TEAM **ENGLAND**

The United captain realised a dream by lifting the Carling Cup, his first trophy as Reds captain, in 2005/06 and went one better in 2007. Accompanied by Ryan Giggs the skipper was presented with the Premiership trophy in front of 76,000 ecstatic fans at Old Trafford, a proud moment for a dyed-in-the-wool United fan. For Neville it was not only a special moment but also the culmination of an impressive 13th season as a first-team regular. The ever-steady right back was vital in the Reds' solid rearguard and remains an automatic choice for both club and country. Injury cut short his contribution to the title-winning season with eight games to go but the team remained strong to be crowned champions. At the age of 32 Gary is regarded as one of the senior stars of Sir Alex's side but has no intention of hanging up his boots any time soon. No sooner was the title won and the skipper was looking to the future. 'Lifting the trophy was an honour,' said Neville, 'but you don't get to celebrate for long. This has to be the beginning. We haven't reached the end of the rainbow with the pot of gold and that's it.' Clearly the United captain is still as hungry as ever and eyeing even more silverware.

DID YOU KNOW?

Gary Neville surpassed legendary goalkeeper Alex Stepney in the appearance stakes in 2007, taking him to fourth in the all-time list of players to have appeared most times for United.

PRIZE GUY

Gary has won more than most in his Reds career:

1995/96 **Premier League, FA Cup**	2000/01 **Premier League**
1996/97 **Premier League**	2002/03 **Premier League**
1998/99 **Champions League, Premier League, FA Cup**	2003/04 **FA Cup**
1999/2000 **Premier League**	2005/06 **Carling Cup**
	2006/07 **Premier League**

John O'Shea

- Born 30 April 1981, Waterford, Ireland
- Signed 3 August 1998, trainee
- Other Clubs None
- United Debut 31 October 1999 v Aston Villa (A) League Cup
- International Team Republic of Ireland

The big Irishman has proven his versatility on a many occasions since bursting onto the scene in 2002. Since his breakthrough season as left back he's played in central midfield, in the centre of defence, at right back and even in goal. Yes, that's right. In 2006/07 John O'Shea deputised for the injured Edwin van der Sar for the last eight minutes of the Reds' 4-0 win at Tottenham Hotspur, Sir Alex having already made his three substitutions. During his brief stint in goal he kept a clean sheet, showing himself as adept at playing as emergency goalkeeper as he is at filling in for outfield players. His displays at right back were impressive in the final weeks of last season and he was one of the players singled out for special praise by Sir Alex following the title success. With age on his side he looks like being a Manchester United player for years to come.

Gerard Pique

- Born 2 February 1987, Barcelona, Spain
- Signed 1 October 2004, trainee
- Other Clubs Barcelona, Real Zaragoza (loan)
- United Debut 26 October 2004 v Crewe Alexandra (A) Carling Cup

Promising young defender Gerard Pique impressed in a season-long loan at Real Zaragoza last term but has now returned to Old Trafford to try to win a place in Sir Alex Ferguson's team. While the Spanish club were keen to make Pique's loan move a permanent one – he also attracted attention from a number of other top clubs – neither the United boss nor the player himself was interested in a deal. Pique has played for the Reds five times in his fledgling career and Sir Alex will be hoping the Catalan defender realises the potential that led him to move for the former Barcelona B team star in 2004. Having experienced a season of top-flight football in Spain Pique will be confident of further improvement this season, with the aim being to prove his value as a squad player and eventually establish himself as a first-team regular.

O'Shea was United's top scoring defender in 2006/07, even popping up with a crucial last-gasp winner at Anfield.

Pique has represented Spain at both Under-19 and Under-21 level and is widely tipped to make the step up to the full squad.

Nemanja Vidic

BORN 21 OCTOBER 1981, UZICE, SERBIA
SIGNED 5 JANUARY 2006, FROM SPARTAK MOSCOW
FEE UNDISCLOSED
OTHER CLUBS RED STAR BELGRADE
UNITED DEBUT 25 JANUARY 2006 v BLACKBURN (H) PREMIERSHIP
INTERNATIONAL TEAM SERBIA

Nemanja Vidic was a real find for United – and his first full season proved exactly why. 'If you go into a 50-50 tackle with Vida then you'll know all about it,' says Wes Brown, who, before Vidic's arrival in January 2006, was considered United's toughest tackler.

The Serbian centre-back has become a fans' favourite for his no-nonsense, rock-solid style. But that toughness isn't his only attribute. Rarely beaten in the air – in defence or attack – he is comfortable on the ball and has struck up an outstanding partnership with Rio Ferdinand. Indeed, the Reds were defeated just twice (away to West Ham and Arsenal) in the Premiership in 2006/07 with Rio and Vida in the side.

Despite taking time to settle after moving from Spartak Moscow, he proved his value last term, even chipping in with four goals. His first for United was typical Vidic, paving the way for victory by powering his header past Wigan goalkeeper Chris Kirkland at the JJB Stadium in October 2006.

To top it off, his displays earned him a place in the Premiership Team of the Year.

DEFENSIVE WARRIOR

'There aren't many players harder than Vida. But what I like is that you know what you'll get every week: a wholehearted performance.'
Rio Ferdinand

'Vida is a hard-tackling defender. He's definitely the toughest-tackling player at the club.'
Wes Brown

'Nemanja is such a brave lad. He's not afraid to put his head in. He's like Steve Bruce in that sense.'
Sir Alex Ferguson

DID YOU KNOW?

As a young player Nemanja initially wanted to be a striker, but his coach thought differently. Thankfully for United, he was told to try playing in defence.

Gabriel Heinze

- **Born** 19 April 1978, Crespo, Argentina
- **Signed** 11 June 2004, from Paris Saint Germain
- **Fee** £6.9million
- **Other Clubs** Newell's Old Boys, Real Valladolid
- **United Debut** 11 September 2004 v Bolton (A) Premiership
- **International Team** Argentina

There are few sights a winger fears more than facing Gabriel Heinze – the Argentina international simply never gives up on winning the ball.

In his first season at Old Trafford, having joined from French club Paris Saint Germain in 2004, he was named Player of the Year by the club's fans. His second term was ruined by a knee injury, but he returned to form with 35 appearances in 2006/07 and was selected ahead of left back rival Patrice Evra for the FA Cup final against Chelsea at Wembley.

His ability to also play in the centre of defence was a major asset to Sir Alex Ferguson, who used him in that position in the season's final stages.

'I know I've given everything I can in every game,' says Gaby, and for that reason he remains a popular figure at United.

'Gaby', as he's known to his team-mates, played only eight games for his first club, Newell's Old Boys, in Argentina before signing for Spanish side Real Valladolid aged 19.

Mikael Silvestre

- **Born** 9 August 1977, Chambray-Les-Tours, France
- **Signed** 2 September 1999, from Internazionale
- **Fee** £4million
- **Other Clubs** Rennes
- **United Debut** 11 September 1999 v Liverpool (A) Premiership
- **International Team** France

Having been at Old Trafford for nearly a decade, Mikael Silvestre is one of the current squad's longest-serving members.

The French full back arrived in 1999 from Internazionale, and although he slipped down the defensive pecking order in 2006/07 – Gabriel Heinze and Patrice Evra shared left back duties, limiting Silvestre to 21 games – he remains as determined and reliable as ever.

A dislocated shoulder in the Champions League win over Lille in March ended his season, but his absence was felt when Evra, Nemanja Vidic, and Rio Ferdinand picked up injuries late on in the campaign. However, Silvestre still played his part, he helped keep out Liverpool in the 1-0 win at Anfield earlier that month and was also one of 19 Reds players to score last term. In a hard-fought match against Watford in August, he expertly fired United's opener in a 2-1 success.

'The manager has faith in me,' he says, 'so I'm looking forward to my ninth season at Old Trafford.'

Mikael has scored ten goals since joining United, but his strike against Watford in 2006/07 was his first away from home for the Reds.

Rio Defenders Ferdinand

BORN **7 NOVEMBER 1978, LONDON**
SIGNED **22 JULY 2002, FROM LEEDS UNITED**
FEE **£30MILLION**
OTHER CLUBS **WEST HAM UNITED**
UNITED DEBUT **27 AUGUST 2003 v ZALAEGERSZEG (H) CHAMPIONS LEAGUE**
INTERNATIONAL TEAM **ENGLAND**

THE UPS AND DOWNS OF RIO FERDINAND

UP July 2002 Signs for United after impressing for England at the 2002 World Cup.

DOWN February 2003 Misses out on his first winner's medal as United lose to Liverpool in the League Cup final in Cardiff.

UP May 2003 Just champion! Rio wins his first Premiership title with United.

DOWN January 2004 The defender begins an eight-month suspension for failing to attend an obligatory drugs test.

UP September 2004 Returns from his ban with an impressive display as United beat Liverpool 2-1 at Old Trafford.

DOWN May 2005 Misses out on another winner's medal as the Reds lose to Arsenal on penalties in the FA Cup final.

UP February 2006 Helps United win the Carling Cup in Cardiff, beating Wigan 4-0.

UP May 2007 Collects his second Premiership winner's medal as the Reds pip Chelsea to the title.

Last season was arguably Rio's best in a red shirt . Alongside Nemanja Vidic he was at the heart of a rock-solid defence that laid the foundations for the Reds' successful title campaign. It was a perfect partnership – Rio providing the silk to the Serbian's steel.

It's a pairing that Rio is delighted to be part of. 'We have a good understanding,' said the world's (still) most expensive defender. 'It's the most settled we've been at the back and we're getting the rewards for that.'

Defensively Ferdinand was as cool as ever. And although not renowned for his scoring, he even weighed in with goals too – scoring against Liverpool at Old Trafford for the second year running. This time the big defender crashed in a superb left foot volley in the 2-0 win against United's fierce rivals, sending the Stretford End into ecstasy.

DID YOU KNOW?

Football may be Rio's first love but it certainly isn't his only one; he also loves music. The Londoner has a wide musical taste and even owns his own record label called White Chalk Music.

Patrice Evra

- **Born** 15 May 1981, Dakar, Senegal
- **Signed** 10 January 2006, from Monaco
- **Fee** Undisclosed
- **Other Clubs** Monza, Nice
- **United Debut** 14 January 2006 v Manchester City (A) Premiership
- **International Team** France

Patrice Evra arrived from Monaco in early 2006 as a lively, attack-minded left back but initially struggled with life in England and the pace of the Premiership. However, following a summer of reflection, settling in and improving his English he was ready for a fresh start to his United career. He was a revelation.

In his first game of the season against Fulham he was defensively assured, energetic yet as attack-orientated as ever, and he never looked back. In fact, he was an almost ever-present in a back four that was virtually unchanged for two thirds of the season, alongside Vidic, Ferdinand and Neville. He now loves life in England. 'Six months ago it was not very good for me, but it was good for my experience, for my head, because every day, every game, every training session I was learning,' says the Frenchman. 'Now I am enjoying it very much.'

United were not the only club interested in signing Evra — at the time he moved to Old Trafford he was also being chased by Liverpool, Arsenal and Italian side Internazionale.

Wes Brown

- **Born** 13 October 1979, Manchester
- **Signed** 8 July 1996, trainee
- **Other Clubs** None
- **United Debut** 4 May 1998 v Leeds United (H) Premiership
- **International Team** England

Wes hails from an area of Manchester called Longsight leading fans to nickname him the 'Longsight Maldini', a reference to his cool defending being similar to that of the Italian international Paolo.

Injuries may have dogged much of Brown's United career but he showed in 2006/07 just how reliable a defender he can be. An excellent marker, tough tackler and a strong header of the ball, Wes is a versatile defender who can play as both full back or as a centre half (his preferred position).

He displayed his full range of attributes in the latter half of the season, filling in for both Gary Neville and Rio Ferdinand. Not bad for a player who has come back from three serious injuries since breaking into the first-team squad as a teenager in 1998 and still made more than 250 appearances for the Reds. His loyalty cannot be faulted, even when sat on the substitute bench. 'When you get called in the main focus is the team and making sure we win,' he said last season. 'To do that you have to play well, and if you play well you get to keep your place.'

Midfielders
Paul Scholes

Paul Midfielders Scholes

BORN **16 NOVEMBER 1974, SALFORD**
SIGNED **8 JULY 1991, TRAINEE**
OTHER CLUBS **NONE**
UNITED DEBUT **21 SEPTEMBER 1994**
v PORT VALE (A) LEAGUE CUP
INTERNATIONAL TEAM **ENGLAND**

A serious eye injury early in 2006 caused doubt over the future of Paul Scholes' career, but he returned last season to produce some of his finest form in a United shirt.

The Reds' league title-winning campaign saw Scholes notch his 500th United appearance, 13 years after making his debut in the League Cup against Port Vale in 1994. And there are few better ways to mark such a milestone than being the game's best player and scoring in a 2-0 win over Liverpool.

His passing, movement and seven goals were a huge influence on reclaiming the title from Chelsea – and only Cristiano Ronaldo's outstanding form bettered Scholesy's contribution. His standout moment in 2006/07 was possibly the precision volley against Aston Villa, when he smashed the ball into the net off the crossbar.

All season he proved that he is still a midfield force to be reckoned with and was voted third by his fellow professionals in the end-of-season PFA Player of the Year awards. The arrival of Owen Hargreaves, Anderson and Nani for almost £50 million will certainly strengthen United next season, but Scholes remains the midfield general.

DID YOU KNOW?

Growing up, Paul was an avid supporter of Oldham Athletic – his idol was former Latics midfielder Andy Ritchie – and he still occasionally attends matches at Boundary Park.

TROPHY CABINET

Scholesy has won a considerable amount of silverware during a 13-year United career:

FA Premier League (7)
1995/96,
1996/97, 1998/99,
1999/2000,
2000/01, 2002/03,
2006/07
FA Cup (3) 1996,
1999, 2004
League Cup (1) 2006
UEFA Champions League
(1) 1999
Intercontinental Cup (1) 1999
Community Shield (4) 1994, 1996,
1997, 2003

30

Michael Carrick

- Born 28 July 1981, Wallsend
- Signed 31 August 2006, from Tottenham Hotspur
- Fee £14million
- Other Clubs West Ham United
- United Debut 23 August 2006 v Charlton Athletic (A) Premiership
- International Team England

Darren Fletcher

- Born 1 February 1984, Edinburgh, Scotland
- Signed 3 July 2000, trainee
- Other Clubs None
- United Debut 12 March 2003 v FC Basel (H) Champions League
- International Team Scotland

In 2006/07 Michael scored three times the number of goals (6) that he scored during his two years with Tottenham Hotspur (2).

In May 2004, Darren captained Scotland in a 1-0 friendly win over Estonia, aged 20, to become his country's youngest captain since John Lambie in a 7-2 victory over Ireland in March 1886.

Taking Roy Keane's old shirt number is not a task many players would relish, but Michael Carrick, completely different in style to the former Reds skipper, quickly made the No.16 jersey his own.

Carrick made a quiet start to his Old Trafford career after his move from Tottenham in 2006, but he ended the season vital to the team. Passing is his outstanding quality and few players, if any, in the Premiership are more accurate. His role is to keep possession and pick out the front players so United can attack quickly and to maximum effect.

Carrick's partnership with Paul Scholes was one of the Reds' many successes in 2006/07. 'Michael's passing is brilliant,' says Scholes. 'He's easy to play alongside because he rarely gives the ball away. He's been a great signing.'

The arrival of Owen Hargreaves adds bite to the midfield, but make no mistake, Carrick will be just as important to the way United play this season.

For Darren Fletcher, 2006/07 was a big season in his development. He started the campaign regularly involved in the starting eleven, but the signing of Michael Carrick and the form of Paul Scholes and Cristiano Ronaldo limited his chances late in 2006.

However, the second half of the season showed just how valuable a player he can be. Energetic, a good passer and always reliable, he also showed he can be versatile, playing on the right wing, at right back and in his favoured central midfield role.

His finest game last season proves he is growing in stature in that role. The headlines in the 2-0 win against Liverpool at Old Trafford in October 2006 belonged to Paul Scholes on his 500th display, but Fletcher helped overpower Steven Gerrard and Momo Sissoko in a crowded midfield to help secure the points.

His efforts are clearly appreciated. 'Darren is a terrific footballer and he is starting to get the credit he deserves,' says Rio Ferdinand.

Owen Hargreaves

Midfielders

BORN **20 JANUARY 1981, CALGARY, CANADA**
SIGNED **1 JULY 2007, FROM BAYERN MUNICH**
FEE **UNDISCLOSED**
OTHER CLUBS **NONE**
INTERNATIONAL TEAM **ENGLAND**

DID YOU KNOW?

Due to his parents' nationality, Owen was eligible to play for England, Scotland, Northern Ireland, Wales, Canada or Germany.

Owen Hargreaves described his move to Old Trafford as 'football's longest-running saga'. There were no less than 324 days from his first being linked with United to signing on 1 July 2007.

Born and raised in Canada, Hargreaves joined Bayern Munich in 1997 aged 16 and, after emerging through the youth ranks, made his debut in August 2000 at the start of a hugely successful season in which Bayern claimed the German league title and the Champions League crown. Owen went on to win three further league titles, three German Cups and one League Cup, scoring ten goals in 211 appearances in seven years at Bayern.

But it was his involvement with the England squad that arguably brought him to United's attention. He was first called into the senior squad in 2001. Although initially a squad player, he came into his own in the 2006 World Cup, earning the Man of the Match award in the quarter-final defeat to Portugal before being voted England Player of the Year in January 2007.

Knowing a host of Reds players through the international set-up should help him settle easily at United, where he will add energy, determination and bite to the midfield to complement the passing and creative skills of Paul Scholes and Michael Carrick.

FACTS AND FIGURES

Here are some more interesting facts about Reds new-boy Owen…

Owen's father Colin played for Bolton Wanderers and Wigan Athletic

In seven years of professional football, he has never received a red card*

Owen made his debut for Bayern Munich aged 19 in August 2000

He scored the first ever goal at Bayern Munich's Allianz Arena stadium in a 3-0 win over Borussia Monchengladbach in August 2005

*Correct at 30 May 2007

Anderson

- ⓔ **Born** 13 April 1988, Porto Alegre, Brazil
- ⓔ **Signed** 1 July 2007, from FC Porto
- ⓔ **Fee** Undisclosed
- ⓔ **Other Clubs** Gremio
- ⓔ **International Team** Brazil

Nani

- ⓔ **Born** 17 November 1986, Amadora, Portugal
- ⓔ **Signed** 1 July 2007, from Sporting Lisbon
- ⓔ **Fee** Undisclosed
- ⓔ **Other Clubs** None
- ⓔ **International Team** Portugal

Anderson – full name Anderson Luís de Abreu Oliveira – won two Portuguese league titles with Porto.

Nani – full name Luís Carlos Almeida da Cunha – scored on his international debut for Portugal against Denmark in September 2006.

In summer 2007, Nani followed in the footsteps of his fellow countryman Cristiano Ronaldo as he made the move from Sporting Lisbon to United.

Much like United's very own wing magician, Nani possesses plenty of pace and likes to run with the ball at defenders. As with Ronaldo, Nani was a product of Sporting's youth system. But, while aged 18 Cristiano had already made the move to Manchester and was testing his skills in the Premiership, at the same age Nani was concentrating on breaking into the Lions' first-team.

His pace immediately caught the eye, as did his ability to go past defenders and his acrobatic goal celebrations.

Nani can play on either the left or right wing and proved in Portugal that he can also score goals, grabbing five in 29 league appearances in 2006/07 while helping his club win the Portuguese Cup.

The signing of FC Porto's skilful Brazilian midfielder Anderson came as a surprise to most United fans. His transfer was announced on the same day as Sporting Lisbon's Nani, but whereas the Portuguese winger had long been linked with a move to Old Trafford, news of Anderson's arrival was unexpected.

Having joined Porto from Gremio in December 2005, he built a reputation as one of the brightest prospects in Portugal despite playing only 21 games for the Dragons. He wasn't completely unknown to Reds supporters, having shone in a pre-season friendly between United and Porto in August 2006.

Anderson is also highly rated in Brazil. He won the Adidas Golden Ball award at the World Under-17 Championships in 2005 as the tournament's most valuable player, and he is tipped to succeed in the senior squad. Brazil coach Dunga says fans at Old Trafford can expect plenty of entertainment, 'Anderson will be a star. He has pace, great footwork and likes to run at opponents. He's a great talent with a terrific attitude and can be one of the best in the world in years to come.'

Ryan Giggs
Midfielders

Manchester United

- BORN **29 NOVEMBER 1973, CARDIFF, WALES**
- SIGNED **9 JULY 1990, TRAINEE**
- OTHER CLUBS **NONE**
- UNITED DEBUT **2 MARCH 1991** v **EVERTON (H) DIVISION ONE**
- INTERNATIONAL TEAM **WALES**

United's current longest-serving player and all-time record medal-winner shows no sign of letting up in his relentless pursuit of silverware. Despite 17 seasons of top-flight football with the Reds – a period in which he's won nine Premiership titles, four FA Cups, two League Cups, the Champions League, the European Super Cup and the Inter-Continental Cup – the Welshman was as impressive as ever last season.

DID YOU KNOW?

The Welshman called time on his international career in June 2007, playing his final match for Wales against the Czech Republic in a Euro 2008 qualifying match. The reason? To help extend his United career.

Whether on the wing, playing as a forward or in the heart of midfield, Giggs displayed all the attributes that make him one of the great British footballers. His pace may have dropped ever so slightly but his dribbling, passing, crossing and eye for an opening remain of the highest order. Sir Alex Ferguson believes he can go on playing for years to come. 'He may be 33 now but he looks after himself and doesn't carry any weight, which is bound to help,' says Sir Alex. 'Ryan will be part of my team next season, there is no question about that. He and Paul Scholes still have a part to play over the next couple of years.' If the boss is correct then there's every chance Ryan could break yet another record – Sir Bobby Charlton's all-time club appearance record. What an achievement that would be.

RECORD BREAKER

Giggs has now won more championship titles than any player in the history of English football:

1992/93 Collects his first title winner's medal
1993/94 A League and Cup double for Ryan
1995/96 Then he's a double Double winner
1996/97 And now a back-to-back champion
1998/99 Then he wins the Treble
1999/2000 Two titles in a row (again)
2000/01 Three in a row this time
2002/03 The title comes home
2006/07 He wins it nine times

Ji-sung Park

- **Born** 25 February 1981, Seoul, South Korea
- **Signed** 8 July 2005, from PSV Eindhoven
- **Fee** £4million
- **Other Clubs** Kyoto Purple Sanga
- **United Debut** 9 August 2005 v Debreceni (H) Champions League
- **International Team** South Korea

Park began his career as a midfielder but was moved to the right wing by former South Korea boss Guus Hiddink.

Ji-sung Park was another player to see his season interrupted by injury but he certainly played his part in the 2006/07 title success. Two goals against Bolton, a crucial third against Blackburn and further strikes against Aston Villa and Charlton kept the Reds on course for the Premiership. But it's not just his goals that make Park such a valuable squad member. On the right-hand side of midfield the Korean is full of energy, playing simple but incisive passes in and around the opposition penalty area. An ankle operation ruled him out in the middle of the season and knee surgery brought his campaign to an end early, but at the age 26 his best years remain ahead of him. 'I still feel I can improve,' says Park. 'I have settled into English life and English football the longer I've been here and there are still areas of my game I want to develop.'

Kieran Richardson

- **Born** 21 October 1984, Greenwich
- **Signed** 2 July 2001, trainee
- **Other Clubs** West Bromwich Albion (loan)
- **United Debut** 23 October 2002 v Olympiakos (A) Champions League
- **International Team** England

The young left-sided midfielder is a product of United's youth academy and played a small but important part in the Reds' Premiership-winning season. A fine crosser with a powerful shot Sir Alex never hesitated in using Richardson on the left wing in the absence of Ryan Giggs.

Kieran's cousin Charley Uchea was a housemate in the 2007 series of reality television show Big Brother.

International recognition has already come his way – he scored twice for England on his debut against the United States – and he enjoyed a successful loan spell at West Bromwich Albion in 2005. Despite being linked with a move to another Premiership club the player sees his future at Old Trafford. 'It would be easy to think about going somewhere else where you're going to play regularly,' says Richardson, 'but somewhere else isn't United.'

Cristiano Ronaldo

Attackers

BORN **5 FEBRUARY 1985, MADEIRA, PORTUGAL**
SIGNED **12 AUGUST 2003, FROM SPORTING LISBON**
FEE **£12.24MILLION**
OTHER CLUBS **NONE**
UNITED DEBUT **16 AUGUST 2003 v BOLTON WANDERERS (H)**
PREMIERSHIP
INTERNATIONAL TEAM **PORTUGAL**

DID YOU KNOW?

Cristiano has one brother, Hugo, and two elder sisters, Elma and Katia, who is a pop star in Portugal known as 'Ronalda'.

STAND-OUT STATS: 2006/07

APPEARANCES/GOALS
Premiership **33/17**
Champions League **11/3**
FA Cup **7/3**
Carling Cup **1/0**
Total **52/23**

FOULS/CARDS
Fouls won **97**
Yellow cards **9**
Red cards **0**

SCORING
Shots on target **64**
Shots off target **78**
Games to goals ratio **2.26**
Most goals in a month
7 (December)

It is surprising to think that Cristiano Ronaldo is in his fifth season at Old Trafford. He arrived in August 2003 as a highly promising but largely unknown talent from Sporting Lisbon, making his eagerly anticipated debut in front of an excited Old Trafford crowd later that month as a substitute against Bolton Wanderers.

At 18, he was skilful but still had a lot to learn. Over the years he has become increasingly more important to United and his pace and breathtaking tricks get Reds fans, neutrals and opposition supporters alike out of their seats, to the point he is now regarded by many as the best player in the world.

Ronaldo's greatest test so far came after being blamed by England fans for their 2006 World Cup exit. He had to show bravery and determination to produce his finest season to date. An incredible 14 individual awards – including two PFA accolades, the Football Writers' gong, plus the Sir Matt Busby and United Players' Player of the Year trophies – marked a wonderful campaign.

Sir Alex Ferguson put it simply, 'He was our star.' His match-winning strike against Fulham in February 2007 was crucial in the title race, and his 23 goals were central to reaching the FA Cup final and Champions League semi-finals in a season where Cristiano proved that, with talent and determination, anything is possible.

Ole Gunnar Solskjaer

- Born 26 February 1973, Kristiansund, Norway
- Signed 29 July 1996, from Molde FC
- Fee £1.5million
- Other Clubs None
- United Debut 25 August 1996 v Blackburn Rovers (H) Premiership
- International Team Norway

Ole Gunnar Solskjaer is one of the most popular players at United, not least for scoring over 100 goals in more than 350 appearances, or his winning goal in 1999's Champions League final, but also because he is one of the club's most dedicated professionals.

The Norwegian had to contend with almost three years out with a knee injury, but he always had the determination to return. His first goal in almost three seasons, against Charlton in August 2006, was an emotional moment for Ole and many United fans who refer to him as a true legend. A further ten goals in 30 appearances followed as he more than played his part in United's successful campaign.

Even when another minor knee operation was required in the summer, Ole was not disheartened. 'Don't write my football career history book yet,' he said, For young footballers there are few better role models.

Ole scored four goals in 11 minutes in United's 8-1 win against Nottingham Forest in February 1999

Giuseppe Rossi

- Born 1 February 1987, New Jersey, USA
- Signed 6 July 2004, from Parma
- Fee Undisclosed
- Other Clubs Newcastle United (loan)
- United Debut 10 November 2004 v Crystal Palace (H) Carling Cup
- International Team Italy

Giuseppe Rossi joined United from Parma at the start of the 2004/05 season, but he ended the 2006/07 campaign back at the Italian club on loan. A young player with great potential, the striker proved that he could cut it against the unforgiving defenders of Italy's top league.

Raised in Clifton, New Jersey, in America, Giuseppe's parents are Italian, which meant he could play for either nation. He chose Italy and has been a regular in the Under-21s since 2006.

Having scored goals for United's reserves as a teenager, Rossi joined Newcastle on loan at the start of last season, but his chances were limited. At Parma, however, he found his form again, scoring nine goals in 19 games to help the Gialloblu avoid relegation.

Despite interest from top clubs in Italy, however, Rossi's intentions remain clear, 'I want to return to United not as the kid in the reserves making the step up, but as a player fully involved in the senior squad. It's where I want to be and where I want to play.'

Wayne Rooney
Attackers

- BORN **24 OCTOBER 1985, CROXTETH**
- SIGNED **31 AUGUST 2004, FROM EVERTON**
- FEE **UNDISCLOSED**
- OTHER CLUBS **NONE**
- UNITED DEBUT **28 SEPTEMBER 2004 v FENERBAHCE (H)** **CHAMPIONS LEAGUE**
- INTERNATIONAL TEAM **ENGLAND**

DID YOU KNOW?

Wayne was barely out of nappies when he started playing football. 'My dad says that at two I was playing football and could volley the ball,' explains the striker.

Pace, power, sublime skill, bags of creativity and an eye for goal – no wonder Wayne Rooney is regarded as one of the best players on the planet. He may have made a slow start to 2006/07 but as the season progressed he was soon displaying his talent on a weekly basis. He ended equal top scorer with Ronaldo on 23 goals and was a key player in the final weeks of the campaign, scoring crucial goals against Bolton Wanderers, Sheffield United and Everton. He's equally devastating as an out-an-out striker or playing in a deeper role. The good news is that Rooney isn't going anywhere soon; he signed a six-year contract extension in November 2006, keeping him at Old Trafford at least until 2012. Sir Alex Ferguson expressed his delight, saying, 'This is great news for everyone at the club. We see Wayne and Cristiano emerging as the best players in the world, they have their finest years in front of them and we'll all be lucky to witness that.'

ROO BEAUTY

Ronaldo may have stolen most of the headlines last term, but Rooney enjoyed plenty of memorable moments:

HAT-TRICK HERO
Bolton 0-4 United
Premiership, Reebok Stadium,
28 October 2006
Rooney ended a supposed 'drought' with three sublime goals – two low shots in the first half, a thumping drive in the second.

CUP KING
Watford 1-4 United
FA Cup, Villa Park,
14 April 2007

Two goals and a stunning all-round display from Rooney helped the Reds reach Wembley – his first was a ferocious 20-yard shot, his second a tap-in.

EURO STAR
United 3-2 AC Milan
Champions League,
Old Trafford,
24 April 2007
The Reds were up against it at Old Trafford, trailing 2-1, but up stepped Rooney to equalise with a deft chip before crashing in an injury-time winner.

MANCHESTER UNITED

Louis Saha

- ⊕ **Born** 8 August 1978, Paris, France
- ⊕ **Signed** 23 January 2004, from Fulham
- ⊕ **Fee** £12.2million
- ⊕ **Other Clubs** Metz, Newcastle (loan)
- ⊕ **United Debut** 31 January 2004 v Southampton (H) Premiership
- ⊕ **International Team** France

Louis missed out on playing for France in the 2006 World Cup final against Italy through suspension, after collecting his second yellow card of the knockout stages in the semi-final against Portugal.

That United were top of the Premiership at the halfway point of the season was thanks in no small part to the goals from Louis Saha. With Ruud van Nistelrooy now at Real Madrid the responsibility of finishing off the team's moves fell to the Frenchman. He didn't disappoint. Three goals in his first five matches got the Reds off to a flying start – his pace, movement and finishing giving United a real threat in attack. At the start of 2007 he'd scored 12 goals and was looking odds-on to finish top scorer. Sadly, injury – something that has blighted his United career – prevented him from playing a major part in the latter half of the season and he ended with 13 goals from 25 starts. Still, Sir Alex remains optimistic that Saha has a real contribution to make, saying, 'Louis has everything. He is quick and brave and gets so many assists.'

Alan Smith

- ⊕ **Born** 28 October 1980, Wakefield
- ⊕ **Signed** 26 May 2004, from Leeds
- ⊕ **Fee** £7million
- ⊕ **Other Clubs** None
- ⊕ **United Debut** 8 August 2004 v Arsenal (N) Charity Shield
- ⊕ **International Team** England

There were few more pleasing sights in 2006/07 than Alan Smith back in the United line-up and tearing around the pitch as if he'd never been away.

Some doubted he would play again following his dislocated ankle and fractured left leg, suffered at Anfield in February 2006. But Smith is made of stern stuff and bravely fought back to play a telling part in the final months of the season. His big chance came against AS Roma in the Champions League and he didn't let anyone down, scoring a superb goal and displaying all the attributes that moved Sir Alex to sign the striker from Leeds in 2004.

Smudger, as he's known to his team-mates, didn't play enough matches to qualify for a Premiership winner's medal. But he still collected one – thanks to the winning club being allowed to apply for medals for players that made a telling contribution.

Determined, strong, superb in the air and with an eye for spectacular strikes... no wonder the boss was pleased to have him back. 'Alan came at a vital time for us,' said Sir Alex. 'He brought enthusiasm and determination, which the other players responded to.'

WORLD AT HIS FEET

Cristiano Ronaldo

Not only did 2006/07 see United walk off with the Premier League trophy but the Reds' Cristiano Ronaldo proved himself one of the world's greatest players. Goals, assists, awards galore... it really was a season to remember for the Portuguese winger. And what's more he's promising more of the same, especially as in April 2007 he signed a new contract to stay at Old Trafford for years to come.

We sat down for a chat with the star of the season to talk about life at United, his big hopes and his ever-lengthening list of awards...

On his new five-year contract
'I am pleased that everything is sorted now. I believe I am at the right club and I am really happy here. The big reason I wanted to stay is to win trophies and because I'm enjoying playing in this team. The spirit is amazing at this club and everyone is playing with confidence.'

On life at United
'I'm happy here with my colleagues, my friends, the coaches and the staff. I am enjoying all of it, everything is good for me. Everyone at Manchester United has

helped me in my short career and I feel like I've improved a lot since arriving here when I was 18. I came here at a young age and I have learned a lot, but I think I can still improve by learning more. This is a good moment for me and I want to keep it going.'

On wearing the famous No. 7 shirt
'When I first arrived at United I said to the boss that I wanted the No. 28 shirt because that was the shirt I wore at Sporting Lisbon for two years. But he said "no, No. 7 is for you". I think at this club the biggest number is No. 7 because there are many great players that have worn it in the past. There is great history in this shirt and there's a responsibility when you wear it. I hope I can keep playing well to honour the shirt.'

On the prospect of being United captain
'The most important thing is playing for such a great club. Being captain isn't something I am aiming to achieve, but one day if I did wear the armband it would be like a dream come true.'

On being Premiership champions
'I think Manchester United now is a different team in many ways because most of the players are older and more mature than in recent seasons. It's the big reason why we performed so well last season and why our results were so good. All the players know each other and know how to play alongside each other because we have played as a team for two or three years now. We have grown together as a team.'

On his United future
'I hope to win trophies, that's what we are aiming to do every season. I hope we can go on to win many more trophies. Personally 2006/07 was a good season for me. I was in good form and enjoying playing for Manchester United. I want to keep that going and always want to do well for my club.'

'I HOPE WE CAN GO ON TO WIN MANY MORE TROPHIES'

On the support of the fans
'For me, United fans are the best supporters in the world because they get behind the team. I think fans at this club appreciate skill, goals and attacking football and that is good because they are the things that I enjoy as well.'

'THERE IS GREAT HISTORY IN THE NO. 7 SHIRT AND THERE'S A RESPONSIBILITY WHEN YOU WEAR IT'

IDOL TALK

Ronaldo is one of the most admired players in modern football with children (and adults) all over the world thrilling at his skills and trickery. Kids in playgrounds from Manchester to Malaysia delight in watching the Portuguese magician at work. But who did the young Cristiano admire when he was growing up?

'When I was young, my idol was Maradona,' says the United star. 'I watched videotapes of him playing and he was a brilliant player. He had such skill and great balance to take the ball past players. He is the most amazing player I have seen play football.' As for what Ronaldo thinks about being an idol to many millions himself? 'It's good to have a reference,' he says, 'somebody you can look to and try to emulate.'

'I THINK I WAS BORN WITH SKILL AND TRICKS BUT I WORK VERY HARD TO TRY AND IMPROVE'

On his role as the entertainer
'I think I was born with skill and tricks. That is natural, but I have to work very hard in training every day – I always have done – to try and improve. The supporters love to see something different, and this is what I try to do. I try to be part of the great things that are done on the pitch. I love to take on defenders and go past them and I think fans like to see that as well. I have a few new tricks but I don't know if I need to introduce them. I try new things in training, but I work on lots of things because that is the only way you can become the best, by working hard. The most important thing is how and when you use your tricks. Knowing when to use your tricks is sometimes the best weapon.'

GONG SHOW

The awards and medals that prove Ronaldo was the 2006/07 man of the season:

On his award-winning season

'I don't approach a season thinking about how well I will do. I am confident in myself and my ability that I have improved last season, but the main thing is that I am enjoying playing for Manchester United, I want to play in every game. When people talk about individual awards, it is good because to be recognised for what you do on the pitch and the contribution you make to the team is a privilege. But awards I receive are not as special as the ones I share with my team-mates. What I wanted more than anything was to win the Premiership. Anything else after that was a bonus.'

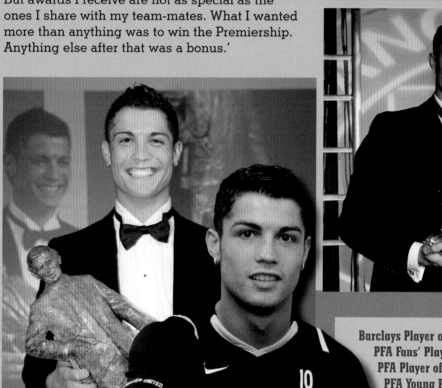

Barclays Player of the Month (November, December)
PFA Fans' Player of the Month (October, February)
PFA Player of the Year
PFA Young Player of the Year
PFA Fans' Player of the Year
PFA Premiership Team of the Year (member of)
Football Writers' Footballer of the Year
Barclays Player of the Season
Portuguese Footballer of the Year
Portuguese Sports Personality of the Year
Sir Matt Busby Player of the Year
Manchester United Players' Player of the Year

SWEEPING THE BOARD

The 2006/07 campaign not only brought the Premier League trophy back to Old Trafford, it was also littered with individual awards for United's players – a just reward for some of the fantastic football played throughout the season. As we've seen, no player gathered quite as many trophies as Cristiano Ronaldo (he picked up 14 individual accolades), but he wasn't the only one...

Barclays Special Merit Award
Ryan Giggs
No player in football league history has won more top-flight titles than United's Welsh winger. Since making his debut in 1991, Giggs has gone on to clinch titles in 1992/93, 1993/94, 1995/96, 1996/97, 1998/99, 1999/00, 2000/01 and 2002/03 before 2006/07's success.

MONTHLY AWARDS
Barclays Player of the Month
Ryan Giggs (August, February),
Paul Scholes (October)

Manager of the Month
Sir Alex Ferguson (August, October, February)

ANNUAL AWARDS
Barclays Manager of the Year 2006/07
Sir Alex Ferguson

PFA Merit Award 2007
Sir Alex Ferguson

GOAL OF THE SEASON

PAUL SCHOLES
v Aston Villa
Villa Park, 23 December 2006

Fans voted in their thousands on ManUtd.com, the Reds' official website, to name Scholes' Christmas cracker against Aston Villa at Villa Park as goal of the season. Gavin McCann headed the ball out of the box but it fell to United's midfield magician, who smashed an unstoppable volley in off the bar.

HE SHOOTS   HE SCORES   HE BAGS THE TROPHY

PFA PREMIERSHIP TEAM OF THE YEAR

People say the league table doesn't lie, but the voting for the Professional Footballers' Association (PFA) Team of the Year tells its own story. United had eight players voted into the team by their fellow Premier League colleagues...

Didier Drogba
Chelsea

Dimitar Berbatov
Tottenham

Ryan Giggs

Steven Gerrard
Liverpool

Paul Scholes

Cristiano Ronaldo

Patrice Evra

Nemanja Vidic

Rio Ferdinand

Gary Neville

Edwin van der Sar

UNSUNG HEROES

WAYNE ROONEY
League appearances 35
Goals 14

The Reds striker may not have claimed a host of individual honours in 2006/07, but his contribution to winning the title was crucial. No United player played more league games than the Englishman and his 14 goals were vital in bringing the Premier League trophy back to Old Trafford.

MICHAEL CARRICK
League appearances 33
Goals 4

After joining from Tottenham in the summer of 2006, Michael Carrick took a little while to settle, but his performances alongside Paul Scholes were central to the Reds' midfield. With a pass completion rate of 83 per cent, Carrick proved a worthy partner for Scholesy, while four league goals doubled his return during two years at Spurs.

JOHN O'SHEA
League appearances 32
Goals 4

The big Irishman scored match-winning goals, filled in at full-back, battled in midfield and even went in goal (keeping a clean sheet after replacing the injured Edwin van der Sar in the 4-0 win over Spurs) during a season in which he showed that it wasn't just the big-name players that helped United win the title.

A FOOTBALLER'S DIET

Trevor Lea

Having the correct food and drink is a crucial part of daily life as a professional footballer. Here, Trevor Lea, United's full-time dietician, discusses the importance of diet for footballers of any age...

What is your role at the club?
'My role is to make sure that all players know what they need to eat and drink to help them train every day and play in games regularly at a highly competative level. It's about educating the players and making sure that, whether in our own canteen at Carrington, or in a hotel for away games, the players have the correct diet.'

What do players eat on an average day?
'They start off with breakfast, generally cereal or toast. After training they have lunch, which consists of carbohydrates (potatoes, noodles, rice, couscous, pasta), a protein food (chicken, pork, turkey, fish, beans), and some vegetables or salad. Size of portion is important. I'd rather the players had more carbohydrates than protein. Throughout the day players need to be drinking plenty, so lots of water or fruit juice. When they go home they will have an evening meal, and maybe a snack – toast or cereal – before they go to bed.'

What is the perfect diet?
'There isn't a perfect diet. Everyone's lifestyle is different, so everyone requires a different diet. Your dietary requirements can change as well. For footballers, it depends on how many games they play in a week, whether they travel away, or if they're returning from injury. The players are learning all the time and they're really focused on diet.'

Is diet as important for young footballers?
'Yes. Your muscles need enough energy to train, play, compete and grow. Muscles have a choice of getting energy from two nutrients: they can metabolise (break down) carbohydrates or fat to release energy for the muscles to do work. Generally, they use both, but the more intense the activity, the more the body prefers to use carbohydrates, which it breaks down in seconds. It's a slower process to break down fat.'

What should a young footballer eat?
'It is essential that a young footballer has a balanced diet to be able to play, train, recover and avoid injury and infection. Balance involves carbohydrate, vegetables, protein, fruit, fat, fibre and water. This sounds tricky but it's basically eating proper meals. The more you train and play the more carbohydrate you need, make sure you eat plenty of rice, potatoes, pasta, noodles, bread and breakfast cereals. Someone with a good nutrition plan for football has three basic meals a day containing complex carbs (like the foods above, which release energy slowly) and maybe some snacks of foods with simple carbs (like bread and jam, malt-loaf, rice pudding, currant buns or low-fat biscuits). You shouldn't go overboard with eating, though. If you eat too much the body will store what it doesn't need by converting it to fat, and that will slow you down. It's also important to have

a five-a-day selection of fruit, vegetables and salads, and also protein, which comes from fish, chicken, pork, beans, peas, lentils, eggs, meats and milk.'

How important is the intake of fluids?

'This is possibly the most important area. Once you start exercising, muscles produce heat, which can damage them. To avoid this the body has a cooling system, part of which is sweating. This means the body loses water, which has to be replaced. To produce sweat the body takes water from the blood, which effectively becomes thicker, like syrup. Thicker blood is harder to pump around the body and so not enough oxygen gets to the muscles. This slows you down physically and also mentally because not as much oxygen gets to the brain. This process of dehydration affects performance, so it's important to learn how much to drink. You get the signs: thirst is one, but another is how often you have to go to the toilet. You should go every two to three hours, indicating that your water volumes in the blood are OK. If you find it's four or five hours since you last went to the toilet, I'd recommend you drink more.'

Is water the best drink?

'Water is what you need. But you can get it from sources other than just drinks. Fruit, like melons, pears, plums, apples and oranges are a good source of water. Fruit juice and smoothies are good, as are squash, cordial and sports drinks. If you're doing long training sessions, you need carbs as well. You can have a drink that contains sugar, like fruit juice or a sports drink, or you could have biscuits and water. That should help you keep performing at your best by maintaining blood sugar and blood volume.'

TRICKS OF THE TRADE

Rene Meulensteen

UNITED CAREER TIMELINE

Name: Rene Meulensteen
Nationality: Dutch
2001: Joins Reds as skills development coach
December 2005: Takes over as United Reserves team coach
April 2006: Completes Reserve League and Manchester Senior Cup double
June 2006: Joins Brondby IF as first team manager
January 2007: Leaves Brondby IF and later returns to United

United's technical skills development coach Rene Meulensteen has some top tips to help improve your game...

What is your role at United?
'I first joined the club in 2001 as skills development coach. At first I worked with players right the way through the club, from the Academy up to the first team. In six years at United [which included a spell away as manager of Danish side Brondby] my role has progressed to the point that I now work with the first team on a daily basis. But I still also have an input into the skill development of the younger players.'

Professional players are already very skilful, do they need to improve their skills?
'Technically, every player can improve, even the best in the world. You can enhance your ability with both feet, improve movement with the ball in both directions, and learn how to deal with specific situations on the field. It's important to practise the skill first then try to relate the work to the player's position on the pitch. With defenders, we concentrate on different skills to the attackers. Attackers use tricks and skills more often than defenders, but we believe that players in every position should be comfortable on the ball.'

What are the United players like to work with?
'They are great. They never have the attitude that "We're already professional footballers so we know everything," absolutely not. They are all very keen to

add to their game. The players here are an absolute privilege to work with, not just because they are fantastic footballers, but also because they are so determined to improve and so willing to learn. That's why they are great role models for young kids.'

Why is learning skills and tricks so important?
'Skills coaching is an area in football that over the years has been underdeveloped. I've spent a lot of my coaching career analysing the best players in the world, and the one thing that makes them stand out – whether it's the best players in our team, or past greats like George Best, Pele, Johann Cruyff or Diego Maradona – they have got a level of skill above their opponents. Look at Cristiano Ronaldo, the tricks he has up his sleeve make him special because he is unpredictable. Defenders don't know what he's going to do.'

What can young players do to improve their game?
'From an early age, young players should learn turns and moves – like the Cruyff turn, stepover, reverse-stepover. The younger you learn the more time you have to practise so that by the time you get older you do them as if they are second nature. If you love football and you have the determination to improve then just enjoy playing and try to be creative. Never be afraid to try new tricks in training even if it doesn't come off. Also, watch your favourite players closely and try to do the things they do. Practice is the key. Being comfortable with the ball at your feet only comes through training, and the more you do it the more you will be able to deal with any situation on the pitch. We always ask the young players at United who they think is the best coach in the world? Most will say Ferguson, but I tell them, "No, you are the best coach" because you have to want to practise and become a better player.'

BEHIND THE SCENES AT
CARRINGTON

Home to United's players and coaching staff – from the first team to the Academy – the Reds state-of-the-art Carrington training base is where the hard work between matches is put in. Here, we get an insider's look at the facilities...

THE MAIN BUILDING

Built on two levels, the main building is used essentially for first team training.

Ground floor
- Training rehab hall with wooden sprung floor
- Weights room
- Swimming pool, hydrotherapy pool, spa pool, sauna and spa rooms
- Three changing rooms for the professional players, four basic Academy changing rooms (used by the Under 18s on Saturday matchdays) and referees' changing room
- Laundry room
- Four kit rooms and one boot room

First floor
- Physio treatment room with ten physio beds
- Doctor's room
- Physio's office, overlooking rehab hall, pools and weights room
- Classroom with computers
- Offices for Academy staff, Coaches, Manager, Manager's PA and charity staff
- Staff canteen (which first team, staff and Academy players all use)
- Players' lounge
- Games room (table tennis, table football, pool)

THE ACADEMY FACILITY

The Academy building was opened in August 2002 and provides training facilities for the club's Under 9s to Under 16s players.

Ground floor
- Indoor training hall with Astroplay pitch
- Eleven changing rooms including coaches' room and referees' room
- Coaches' briefing room
- Boot-wash area
- Three-bed treatment area
- Physio's office
- Outdoor floodlit Astroplay pitch

First floor
- Parents lounge
- Indoor and outdoor viewing balconies
- Two interview rooms
- Training room

FACTS AND FIGURES

- The complex cost around £22million to build. The main building – where the first team and staff are based cost £14million, with the separate Academy building costing a further £8million.

- The Trafford Training Centre is based in Carrington and is set on a site of 108 acres, 85 acres of which are used by the club. The remaining land is rented to a local farmer and there is also a small nature reserve, which is managed as a joint partnership between the club and the Cheshire Wildlife Trust.

- The training ground was opened in January 2000 when United moved from the old Cliff Training Ground.

- There are twelve grass pitches on the site. Two of the pitches have undersoil heating and are used by the first team.

A TRUE UNITED LEGEND

Ryan Giggs

The most decorated player in United's history, Ryan Giggs has Sir Bobby Charlton's all-time appearance record of 759 games within sight, and he isn't about to slow down his pursuit of more silverware and more matches in the red shirt. Having held aloft the Premier League trophy (alongside skipper Gary Neville) for a record ninth time last term, Ryan guides us through the 2006/07 campaign, looks back on his career so far and discusses what the future holds…

'The satisfaction of last season's title was really high…
The standard required to win the league is so much higher now than in previous years. Since we last won it in 2003, the bar has been raised, first by Arsenal and then by Chelsea. We have a relatively young squad and there aren't too many players that have won it before. It's always nice for the younger lads, like Wayne Rooney and Cristiano Ronaldo, but also for the other lads who've joined recently; Nemanja Vidic, Patrice Evra and Ji-sung Park. The one thing the manager offers his players is trophies, and the winning feeling is always great.'

'I knew we were good enough to win it…
I was certain we could compete and I knew that if we got off to a good start then we had the experience to go all the way. There are so many twists and turns in the title race, but that's where the knowledge of the manager and the experience of the older lads comes in. We had a squad that was potentially very good, but

RYAN'S FACTS AND FIGURES: 2006/07

APPEARANCES
League 30
Champions League 8
FA Cup 6
Total 44

GOALS
League 4
Champions League 2
FA Cup 0
Total 6

BEST GAME
Watford 1 United 2
Vicarage Road, 26 August 2006
The Welshman got off to a flier at the start of the season and as captain on his 600th start his match-winning performance was one of many as the season developed.

BEST GOAL
Fulham 1 United 2
Craven Cottage, 24 February 2007
Latching onto Wayne Rooney's lofted pass, Giggs struck his volley with precision on the outside of his boot, equalising before Cristiano Ronaldo did his stuff late on to secure a crucial victory at the start of the run in.

BEST GAME

BEST GOAL

you've got to take that next step and prove you can win trophies. Everyone could see the promise this team had, but we had to prove how good we were. We've done that now, and hopefully it gives us the platform to go on and win more trophies.'

'Seeing the look on the younger lads' faces was great...
That was one of the first things I thought about when I knew we'd won the title – seeing the look on their faces. I know how I felt when I won my first title in 1993, it was brilliant. It brought all those memories flooding back. Like then, winning it last season was a huge team effort. There's a real togetherness in the squad and everyone played their part. We all feel like we made a contribution to it.'

'Beating Chelsea to the title was a huge challenge...
Chelsea can buy any player they want, and when they're all fit they could put two teams out – and two quality teams at that. We were lucky that they had a few injuries, while we were reasonably OK in terms of injuries up until the final few weeks. But I think we were due that bit of luck because we've had injuries in that past few seasons and that's really worked against us. But we certainly made the most of it this time.'

'Ronaldo was outstanding, but so was the team...
'I normally don't like to pick players out, but the way Cristiano was consistently good – for such a young player as well – made him stand out. He was brilliant all season. As a winger, you rely on players getting you the ball in the right positions. It's hard to maintain your consistency, but he did that and everyone recognised it. But the real reason we were so good is that, as a team and as a squad, every player contributed.'

THE LIFE OF RYAN

Ryan takes us through his United career, from starting out, the lows, the highs and the future…

The story begins…

It seems astonishing to think that Ryan Giggs made his United debut almost 17 years ago, against Everton at Old Trafford in March 1991. 'I remember Les Sealey (former goalkeeper) telling me I was a substitute and when I replaced Denis Irwin, who was injured, I wasn't nervous at all really.' But it was his first full start against Manchester City a few weeks later that really caused a fuss. 'I'll always remember the manager saying, "Ryan, you're playing on the left". I enjoyed the game and was credited – luckily – with the winning goal.'

An early low…

Fortunately for Giggs the highs in his career significantly outweigh the lows, but one low point has always stayed with the Welshman. 'Losing the title at Anfield in April 1992 was terrible,'

he says. 'Leeds won in the morning, so we had to beat Liverpool on their patch to keep our hopes of winning the league alive. We lost 2-0, confirming Leeds as champions. All of Anfield celebrated, taking pleasure from our disappointment. Even now, that memory helps motivate me when we play Liverpool.'

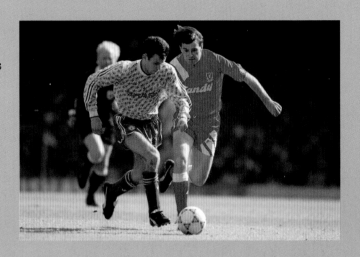

Scoring 'that goal'…

The sight of a Giggs charging down the Villa Park touchline waving his shirt in the air sends a tingle down the spine. His extra-time winner against Arsenal in the 1999 FA Cup semi-final was nothing short of unbelievable. He recalls, 'It's the best goal I've scored because of the occasion. It kept our Treble hopes alive. When I cut out that pass from Vieira, I didn't realise I was in my own half. There was no one in front of me, so I just put my head down and went towards goal. There was no way I was going to pass it. I skipped past Vieira, then Dixon and Vieira again. I was then in between Dixon and Keown, who didn't want to tackle me as I was near the area. I got past them and hit it as hard as I could past David Seaman. My celebrations show how much that goal meant to me and the team.'

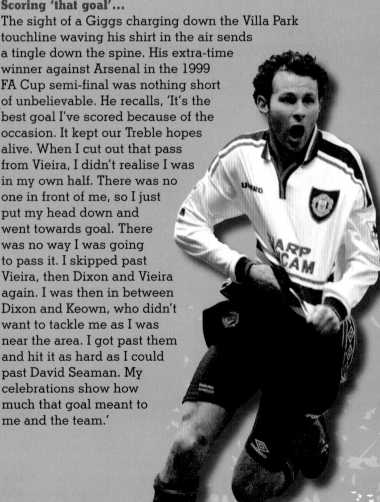

Tears of joy...

'For years I'd watched players on television collecting trophies and always thought, "What are they crying about?" I was certain I would never, ever do that,' recalls Giggs. But the high drama of 1999's Champions League triumph, the final jewel in the Treble crown was no ordinary experience. 'When the final whistle went at the Nou Camp, I just dropped to my knees and started crying, I couldn't help it,' he says. 'The emotion of winning was so overwhelming.'

Personal best...

The Treble season was hard to beat, but United followed it up with another title success, the second of three in a row, and Giggs was on fire. 'I look back on the 1999/2000 season as the best of my career,' he said. 'After Christmas I reached a level of performance and consistency I'd not known before. Sir Alex spoke to me about concentrating on what I do best – taking players on at pace. I realised what he was saying and tried to put it into practice. I tried to take more players on and I really enjoyed it.'

Title number nine and the future...

'It felt really special to win the title last season,' says Giggs, 'but I'm not thinking of it as my ninth, I'm just glad United have won it having gone three years without it.'

That attitude is a sign of Giggs' professionalism and dedication to winning for the team rather than himself. But there is no reason why he can't extend his record title-winning haul and make it ten. 'I'm enjoying us being known as champions, and all I want to do now is win it again.'

THE THEATRE

- The expansion of United's magnificent Old Trafford stadium means the ground's capacity stands at a staggering 76,212.

- United have topped the attendance list every season since the Premier League's inception, except 1992/93 when the Stretford End was undergoing redevelopment.

- Last season also saw record season ticket figures, with more than 50,000 Reds attending every league home game.

- There are 142 turnstiles in operation on matchdays.

- There are 15 ball boys at every match, each one a year-ten student at a local school.

OF DREAMS

- On matchdays the stadium's catering staff prepare over 5,000 meals.

- Fans have access to 72 kiosks around the ground, which sell an average of 20,000 bottles of beer per match.

- The ground boasts 165 executive boxes, which can accommodate 1,262 people.

- The car parks at the stadium accommodate 5,200 vehicles.

- More than 200,000 fans visit the United museum each year.

- Stadium tours are most popular during July and August. During these times, the guides can conduct up to 42 tours a day, spaced 10 minutes apart and with 35 people in each group.

- The pitch is 105 metres long and 68 metres wide. It takes two members of the groundstaff one-and-a-half hours to cut the grass, which is done daily in summer and three times a week during the winter.

- The distance from the ground to the highest steel support on North Stand is a massive 48.5 metres.

- Safety is important at Old Trafford, and should the stadium need to be evacuated in an emergency it would take just eight minutes to empty entirely.

THE GREAT UNITED QUIZ

Think you're a bit of a brain box when it comes to knowledge about United? Do you know which Scottish giant Sir Alex used to play for; or in which year the Reds first won the League Cup? Put your United knowledge to the test with our fun quiz pages...

NAME GAME

Can you work out the names of the ten United players that have been scrambled below?

A FRIED ROD INN	ORLANDO
BE SENT FOR	ACE RAVE TRIP
CAN INVADE JIM	AN EYE WON ROY
A WASH GREEN OVER	SONAR DEN
A REVEL LYING	CALL SUE POSH

TRUE OR FALSE?

1. Wayne Rooney and Cristiano Ronaldo were joint top scorers in 2006/07.

2. Anderson is the first Brazilian to play for Manchester United.
3. Sir Alex Ferguson used to play for Glasgow Celtic.
4. Owen Hargreaves was born in London, England.
5. Nani scored direct from a corner on his debut for Portugal.

WHO AM I?

1. This record-breaking Premiership medal-winner retired from international football in 2007 after winning 64 caps for his country. Born in his nation's capital city he moved to Manchester in childhood and after signing for the Reds made his debut in the 1990/91 season. He has since played over 700 times for the Reds.
2. This midfielder of vast experience is another to have called time on his international career earlier than expected. As a teenager he made his United debut against Port Vale in the League Cup, scoring twice. Last season he scored against Liverpool in his 500th United appearance.
3. Having signed a new contract in August 2006 this former Rennes defender was described by the United manager Sir Alex Ferguson as, 'an important member of the squad for seven years now.' Though injury cut short his season last time out, he can play as both centre half and left back.
4. This former West Bromwich Albion player was a member of his country's squad for the Germany 2006 World Cup but did not feature. That summer he moved to Old Trafford from the Hawthorns and made 13 appearances for the Reds in 2006/07.

IN THIS YEAR...
Name the year each of the following things happened.
1. Eric Cantona retired from football aged 30.
2. United won the League Cup for the very first time.
3. Wayne Rooney was born.
4. Newton Heath LYR was formed, the club that was renamed Manchester United.

SPOT THE BALL
Study this action shot from the 2006/07 season and tell us from which square we have removed the ball.

GOAL CRAZY
1. Against which team did Wayne Rooney score United's only hat-trick of 2006/07?
2. How many penalties did Ronaldo score last season?
3. Who scored United's first goal of 2007?

GUESS WHO?
United players are instantly recognisable to football fans all over the world, but can you identify the players pictured below?
1. Sir Alex likes to keep an eye on things, but which Reds defender is it getting his special attention here?
2. Whose turn is it to feel the steel in this tackle by Nemanja Vidic?

3. Who is it making sure his head is out of the way of Michael Carrick's pass?
4. His performances in training have been impressive, but who is this player leading the reserves a merry dance?

Answers

Who am I?
1. Ryan Giggs
2. Paul Scholes
3. Mikael Silvestre
4. Tomasz Kuszczak

In this year...
1. 1997
2. 1992
3. 1985
4. 1878

Spot the ball
Ball is in square 47

QUICKFIRE QUIZ

Goal crazy
1. Bolton Wanderers
2. Five
3. Paul Scholes, v Newcastle United (A)

Guess who?
1. Nemanja Vidic
2. Darren Fletcher
3. Paul Scholes
4. Giuseppe Rossi

THE GREAT UNITED QUIZ

Name game
Rio Ferdinand, Ronaldo, Ben Foster, Patrice Evra, Nemanja Vidic, Wayne Rooney, Owen Hargreaves, Anderson, Gary Neville, Paul Scholes

True or false?
1. True, they both scored 23 goals
2. False, Kleberson was United's first Brazilian
3. False, he played for Glasgow Rangers
4. False, he was born in Calgary, Canada
5. True, against Denmark on 1 September 2006

Fixtures 2007/08

AUGUST 2007

scorers

| Sun 12 (H) | MANCHESTER UNITED |
| 4.00p.m. | READING |

scorers

scorers

| Wed 15 (A) | PORTSMOUTH |
| 7.45p.m. | MANCHESTER UNITED |

scorers

scorers

| Sun 19 (A) | MANCHESTER CITY |
| 1.30p.m. | MANCHESTER UNITED |

scorers

scorers

| Sun 26 (H) | MANCHESTER UNITED |
| 4.00p.m. | TOTTENHAM HOTSPUR |

scorers

SEPTEMBER 2007

scorers

| Sat 1 (H) | MANCHESTER UNITED |
| 5.15p.m. | SUNDERLAND |

scorers

scorers

| Sat 15 (A) | EVERTON |
| 12.00p.m. | MANCHESTER UNITED |

scorers

scorers

| Sun 23 (H) | MANCHESTER UNITED |
| 4.00p.m. | CHELSEA |

scorers

scorers

| Wed 26 | |
| Carling Cup 3rd Rd | |

scorers

scorers

| Sat 29 (A) | BIRMINGHAM CITY |
| 5.15p.m. | MANCHESTER UNITED |

scorers

OCTOBER 2007

scorers

| Sat 6 (H) | MANCHESTER UNITED |
| 12.45p.m. | WIGAN ATHLETIC |

scorers

scorers

| Sat 20 (A) | ASTON VILLA |
| 5.15p.m. | MANCHESTER UNITED |

scorers

scorers

| Sat 27 (H) | MANCHESTER UNITED |
| | MIDDLESBROUGH |

scorers

---

scorers

| Wed 31 | |
| Carling Cup 4th Rd | |

scorers

NOVEMBER 2007

scorers

| Sat 3 (A) | ARSENAL |
| 12.45p.m. | MANCHESTER UNITED |

scorers

scorers

| Sat 10 (H) | MANCHESTER UNITED |
| | BLACKBURN ROVERS |

scorers

scorers

| Sat 24 (A) | BOLTON WANDERERS |
| | MANCHESTER UNITED |

scorers

DECEMBER 2007

scorers

| Sat 1 (H) | MANCHESTER UNITED |
| | FULHAM |

scorers

scorers

| Sat 8 (H) | MANCHESTER UNITED |
| | DERBY COUNTY |

scorers

scorers

| Sat 15 (A) | LIVERPOOL |
| 12.00p.m. | MANCHESTER UNITED |

scorers

scorers

| Wed 19 | |
| Carling Cup 5th Rd | |

scorers

scorers

| Sat 22 (H) | MANCHESTER UNITED |
| | EVERTON |

scorers

scorers

| Wed 26 (A) | SUNDERLAND |
| | MANCHESTER UNITED |

scorers

scorers

| Sat 29 (A) | WEST HAM UNITED |
| | MANCHESTER UNITED |

scorers

JANUARY 2008

scorers

| Tue 1 (H) | MANCHESTER UNITED |
| | BIRMINGHAM CITY |

scorers

scorers

| Sat 5 | |
| FA Cup 3rd Rd | |

scorers

scorers

| Wed 9 | |
| Carling Cup Semi-final 1st leg | |

scorers

scorers

| Sat 12 (H) | MANCHESTER UNITED |
| | NEWCASTLE UNITED |

scorers

scorers

| Sat 19 (A) | READING |
| | MANCHESTER UNITED |

scorers

scorers

| Wed 23 | |
| Carling Cup Semi-final 2nd leg | |

scorers

scorers

| Sat 26 | |
| FA Cup 4th Rd | |

scorers

scorers

| Wed 30 (H) | MANCHESTER UNITED |
| | PORTSMOUTH |

scorers

FEBRUARY 2008

scorers

| Sat 2 (A) | TOTTENHAM HOTSPUR |
| | MANCHESTER UNITED |

scorers

scorers

| Sun 10 (H) | MANCHESTER UNITED |
| 12.00p.m. | MANCHESTER CITY |

scorers

scorers

| Sat 16 | |
| FA Cup 5th Rd | |

scorers

scorers

| Sat 23/Sun 24 | |
| Newcastle United (A) †/Carling Cup final* | |

scorers